Mind Time

Michael Chaskalson & Megan Reitz

Thorsons

Thorsons
An imprint of Harpercollins*Publishers*
1 London Bridge Street
London SE1 9GF

www.harpercollins.co.uk

1 2 3 4 5 6 7 8 9 10

A catalogue record of this book is
available from the British Library

ISBN: 978-0-00-825280-9

Printed and bound in Great Britain by
CPI Group (UK) Ltd, Croydon, CR0 4YY

MIX
Paper from
responsible sources
FSC
www.fsc.org   FSC® C007454

This book is produced from independently certified FSC paper
to ensure responsible forest management.

For more information visit: www.harpercollins.co.uk/green

Michael
For Annette –
and for Ellie, Chloe, Ollie and Scarlett

Megan
For Steve, Mia and Lottie –
and John, Rachel and Doug Goodge

AIM

Allowing
Inquiry
Meta-awareness

Contents

Introduction

Your mind is extraordinary. *Your* mind. The mind that, right now, sees black marks on white paper and effortlessly turns them into bundles of meaning. The same mind that sees the word 'sunset' and fluently converts it into an inner vision of colours and shades. Without even trying.

How extraordinary. How miraculous.

To perform its amazing feats, your mind has an information-processing capacity greater than the combined power of all the computers, routers and Internet connections on Earth. Did you know, for example, that a tiny piece of your brain, the size of a grain of sand, contains 100,000 neurons and 1 billion synapses all communicating with each other.[1] The brain is the mind's supercomputer. It can connect 100 trillion bits of information.

So with this amazing capacity available to us, how do we use our minds?

The simple answer is, not as well as we might. For a start, about half the time we are awake we are thinking about something other than what is going on at the time.[2] And we keep trying to multitask – ordering a pizza while walking the dog and Skyping a cousin in Australia. Recent research, however, shows multitasking significantly reduces our overall performance.[3]

Then there are all the things our minds do on autopilot. Do you wake up in the morning and reach for your phone, blearily checking your emails while still lying in bed? Do you sit in traffic on your way to work scowling when someone beeps their horn, without even considering that they might be trying to tell you something useful?

The fact is that we are only aware of a tiny fraction of what we are thinking, feeling and sensing – so we're barely conscious of how and why we behave the way we do. It's as if we have a large, elegant, state-of-the-art ocean-going cruise liner at our command and all we use it for is chugging about the harbour.

The problem is that although we have all that enormous potential at our disposal, our minds don't come with an instruction manual. As miraculous as they are, we don't know how to use them to anything like their full capacity. All we get is some rudimentary guidance.

We've all been educated to some extent. We've learned to do calculations and construct sentences; we've maybe learned history, geography, science, technology, languages or commerce. We can cook and shop, work the Internet and drive a car. We can do our jobs. We might even have mastered some of these to a very high level. But it's not the same. We still don't use or direct our minds effectively. And that affects the way we relate to others, the way we feel, the way we think and the way we experience the world around us.

Most of the time our minds just run on automatic and we're barely aware that they're doing that. This keeps us confined in the narrow space of our habits. Mentally, emotionally and in our behaviours, we keep doing what we've always done – and we keep getting what we've always got. Sometimes we manage to break out into new ways of doing things. But often, with a sad predictability, these new resolutions and good intentions don't last and we flip back to automatic again.

That's the bad news. The good news is that we can do so much better, and it's not that hard. We just need to know how to use our minds more effectively.

This book sets out to help you get your mind out of automatic more often. The training programmes we've led throughout the world and our research tell us that it's possible for us all to do this – and when we do so life goes much better. We become more resilient, we have stronger relationships and we're better able to manage unexpected events. We feel more awake, more alive and more creative. And that's because we are!

Everything that happens as we go about our day shapes and changes our minds in subtle (or less subtle) ways. A difficult telephone call leaves us feeling a bit low; a cheerful remark leaves us feeling more buoyant. The mind is a kind of liquid lens. It's always moving and changing, and as it shifts the world that it perceives also shifts. There are still houses, streets and trees out there, but the quality of our experience alters.

The important point is this. You can leave that process to chance, letting your mind be randomly shaped and changed by passing events, or you can get more involved in the process and help to direct it. There are simple things you can do every day to help you shape your mind so that whatever life brings you're better able to respond creatively.

And the even better news is that it only takes 10 minutes a day. Yes, just 10 ... short ... minutes. We call that Mind Time, and we all need it.

If you can set aside 10 minutes each day to engage in a few simple practices,and if you really follow the advice we've given about doing them, then in a few months things should get better. That's our promise to you. But you have to commit the 10 minutes of your day. No one else can do that for you.

The fact that you picked up this book suggests that you are looking for something to make your life better. The question is: are you ready to embark on a fascinating and – literally – mind-expanding journey? We hope so. The upside is huge.

We will introduce you to your own mind so that you can begin to see more clearly how it works. We'll show you some of the levers you can pull so that you can begin to shape your mind more as you want it. We'll teach you how to stand back a little – just a tiny bit – so that you can see what your mind is up to more often, and that will allow you to make more powerful choices about where you want it to go.

In the first chapter, we'll lay out the problem more fully and suggest some solutions. We'll discuss the research we conducted and introduce some simple practices that you can do every day. These will help you develop three key capacities, which we collectively refer to as 'AIM':

1. **Allowing** – an attitude of kindness and acceptance.
2. **Inquiry** – a curiosity about your present-moment experience.
3. **Meta-awareness** – the ability to observe your thoughts, feelings, sensations and impulses as they are happening and see them as temporary and not 'facts'.

AIM will help you to become more alive and aware of yourself, of others and of the world around you. And that greater awareness gives you more choices. That's what AIM is all about – choiceful response rather than choiceless reaction.

The elements of AIM are mapped out in Chapter 1. Allowing and Inquiry are more easily understood – though the devil is in the practice. Meta-awareness is more obviously challenging. 'Meta' means 'beyond' or 'at a higher level'. So we are referring to a specific type of awareness. It describes a particular way of *observing* and being able to *describe* what is happening in the ever-changing stream of your experience from moment to moment. This is explained more fully in Chapter 1.

Chapter 2, 'Learning to AIM', discusses the Mind Time practices that will help you to shape your mind and shows you how to access the audio recordings, which guide you through these practices.

In many ways Chapter 2 is the heart of the book. When you've read it, we encourage you to begin straight away with the Mind Time practices. And keep doing them. The benefits on offer take time to emerge.

In the chapters after that we'll look at how you can apply some of the skills you'll learn to key parts of your life.

We'll look at:

- AIM for better relationships (Chapter 3)
- AIM for happiness (Chapter 4)
- AIM for effective working (Chapter 5)
- AIM for better health (Chapter 6)
- AIM for work–life balance (Chapter 7)
- AIMing when times are tough (Chapter 8)

Then we round things up and leave you with some final inspiration.

Our minds are the key to unlocking the life we wish to lead. The state of our minds not only directly affects *our* happiness, learning, creativity and performance, it affects the happiness, learning, creativity and performance of those around us: our family, friends and colleagues. The state of our mind determines our experience of life and deeply influences the experiences those around us have.

Isn't it time we learned to shape our minds – not be shaped by them? We think so, and this book will show you how.

Michael Chaskalson and Megan Reitz
June 2017

Chapter 1

Why AIM?

Imagine …

You're sitting around the table at a family gathering. Everyone's there: your parents, your partner, your kids, your brother and sister. It's all been wonderfully good humoured and everyone's having a good time. But then a subject comes up that sparks old tensions between your mother and your brother.

Your mother comments; your brother bristles and retorts.

Your mum sits up straighter in her chair and replies crossly. And they're off.

It's a familiar pattern. The rest of you silently, awkwardly, look on – and vainly try to steer the conversation towards something lighter.

You feel tense, upset and resigned, caught up in a family argument that's been around for years and may be around for many years to come. You're annoyed with your mum and brother. You wish they'd just sort this out. You're fed up with the emotional rollercoaster that comes with these situations and you say to yourself that maybe it's best to avoid these gatherings from now on.

However, it doesn't have to be like this.

You can't change your mum, your brother and the dynamic between them. But you can change how *you* are in the situation

– and that can change everything. With AIM – Allowing, Inquiry and Meta-awareness – you experience things differently.

Here's how it works.

Allowing has two sides to it. There's a wisdom side and a compassion side.

With the wisdom side, you let what *is* the case *be* the case. This means recognising that this moment – this very moment, right now – couldn't be anything other than it is. You can't go back in time and change things so that this moment somehow turns out to be different. Right now, it is what it is. And it's only when you can truly allow that it is what it is that you have choice about what to do next.

So, with your mum and your brother, you recognise that it is what it is. This is what it's like and there's no sense in wishing it could magically be different right now.

We spend so much of our time wishing that things weren't as they are. 'If only I were different' or 'if only they were different' or 'if only my work was different, or I had more money, or I was better looking, or fitter, or …' Anything, really. None of that helps. It is what it is. And when we can allow that, we begin to have some real choice about what we do next.

This moment can't be changed, but the next moment is undecided. What we do now shapes what comes next, and when our actions are rooted in allowing and acknowledging the current reality of things then they're very much wiser and more effective.

So part of the first step with AIM in this particular family situation is to allow that it is actually what it is. But this isn't cold and indifferent, because as well as a wisdom side to Allowing, there's also a compassion side.

Compassion involves being kinder and more accepting towards everyone involved in each situation – yourself and others. In this case, it might mean seeing with care and concern all the unhappiness that your mum and your brother are inflicting on themselves as they act out this familiar drama. And it means being kind and concerned for everyone else involved in the moment, including yourself.

Compassion needs to start with yourself. That often goes against our assumptions about what compassion or kindness is all about. But when we're better able to be kind to ourselves it can help us be kinder to others.

It's so easy, and so common, to be harshly self-critical. We can sometimes speak to ourselves in ways we'd never speak to others. 'Where did I leave my keys? Oh, that's so stupid! I've lost them again. I keep doing that. That's so stupid. I'm such an idiot!' If your friend told you she'd lost her keys and you used that kind of language to her, she'd think it very odd.

With Allowing we're kinder to ourselves. And we're kinder and more accepting of others. Everyone has their own history that has shaped them to be as they are. We're all doing our best to make a life and to get by. Yes, some people can annoy us. Some can seem harsh and unkind. But if we really understood what it's like from their side – what it's like to be them – maybe we'd be less critical. With Allowing, we ease back a bit on our own harsh and critical judgements – towards ourselves, others and the situations we find ourselves in.

So, in the case of your mum and your brother, you allow the experience, in that moment, to be what it is.

You don't get angry with yourself for letting the situation get to you. You don't get angry with the others around the table – that wouldn't help. And instead of helplessly wishing things were different you're able to accept that it is what it is. Like it or not, what is happening *is* happening.

The second part of AIM is **Inquiry**.

Inquiry involves taking a lively interest in each moment of experience. As you develop your capacity for Inquiry you find yourself occupying an increasingly interesting world. You begin to notice what's happening inside you, your thoughts, feelings, body sensations and impulses – right now. And you get more interested in what's happening outside you, in the world around you, right now. You get more interested in other people – what's going on for them? And you get more interested in what's happening between you and others – the constantly changing, endlessly fascinating dynamic of humans relating to each other.

With Inquiry, the rich and complex tapestry of this present moment lights up. You become more alive to each moment and begin to see more into the depth of things.

Coming back to the situation at that family gathering, instead of reacting you begin to inquire. You broaden your attention. Rather than being lost in what is happening out there – as if you're immersed in a TV show, emotionally at the mercy of what happens next – you become interested in your experience. You begin to wonder what the others around the table might be experiencing. You notice things in the space around you that might be influencing what's happening.

Questions form in your mind: 'What am I feeling right here and now?' 'What do I see in the faces of my family?' 'What *is* the atmosphere in the room right now?' 'What am I seeing that can give me a clue about what this strange dynamic is all about?'

You're open, engaged and interested. Alive to what's happening. Caring, kind and curious.

And you have **Meta-awareness**, the third element of AIM.

You are simultaneously 'in' your experience, feeling and sensing what's going on, and at the same time you're able to notice some of the ways it's unfolding for you.

You notice and can, to some extent, describe your thoughts, feelings, body sensations and impulses as they arise and pass. The lens of your awareness can be set narrower, focused just on yourself and your inner experience, and it can be set wider. You can pay attention outside yourself – you pick up your relations' body language and facial expressions. You notice how warm the room is and how the music in the background is quite lively and fun, in contrast to the mood in the room.

Meta-awareness is a way of experiencing that we all have to some extent. And it's something that we can develop much further. Here's an example that might help you to understand a little better what we mean by meta-awareness.

If you have ever travelled on the London Underground at rush hour you will be familiar with this experience. You're standing on a station platform at 5.30 p.m. It's hot and crowded. It's been a tough day and you're feeling frazzled. You can't wait to get home, take off those shoes, get a drink and relax. A train pulls in. People struggle to get off – there's hardly any space on the crowded platform – and others rush to get on. Pushed from behind, you just make it. You're standing there, hot, breathless, squeezed from all sides as the train pulls out. There hardly seems to be room to breathe. You grow increasingly irritated.

'Oh no. This is intolerable!' you think. 'Why am I doing this to myself? People are so inconsiderate! If another person pushes their backpack into my face I swear I'll scream! In the morning they all stink of aftershave. In the evening it's body odour. This is ridiculous! It's completely intolerable ...'

And on and on.

That's one way of being with what's happening.

Here's another. You start to grow irritable, but meta-awareness kicks in. You notice that your jaw is tight and that you're holding your shoulders up so they're almost alongside your ears. You see that your thoughts and feelings have fallen into 'unhelpful inner-rant' mode.

So you ease your jaw, relax your shoulders and come away from the rant. 'Gosh – I'm having such irritable thoughts!'

In this instance, the difference is between *being irritable* and *noticing* that you're having irritable thoughts and feelings.

That moment of stepping back, ever so slightly, of seeing what you're up to and what's going on, is a tiny shift – but it changes everything.

One moment you're unconsciously 'doing irritation' – lost in your inner rant, treating the world as if it were intolerable (it's not – you do this commute every day, it must be tolerable). The next moment you wake up to what you're doing and you begin to exercise some choice. You can ease your jaw, relax your shoulders, at least to some extent, and you can stand there and be with the discomfort of the moment knowing that it won't last for more than a few minutes. Perhaps you recognise that this is part of the price you pay for living in such a vibrant city with so many great opportunities.

Meta-awareness involves waking up to what's going on with us – with our thoughts, our feelings, our body sensations and impulses – in each moment. When we have that awareness, then we can choose what we do next. When we don't have it, we're stuck in the rut of our familiar, habitual reactions.

• •

When Allowing, Inquiry and Meta-awareness come together, in any combination, they open up a space in which we're able to respond, rather than react, to whatever situation we find ourselves in. Remember, AIM is all about choiceful response rather than choiceless reaction.

AIM lets you sit at that table with your family much more resourcefully. You see what's going on in a much richer way. That lets you make choices. You can choose to intervene in a skilful, caring way if that seems possible. Or you can choose not to if the opportunity isn't there. But whatever you do or don't do, your response comes from a sensitive, kindly and informed choice. AIM is the exact opposite of the unconscious reaction that keeps family dynamics like this endlessly spinning.

It's important to realise, though, that AIM is not the same as being dispassionate. Just because we don't get caught up in the familiar patterns of reactivity playing out around us doesn't mean we don't feel for what's going on. It doesn't mean we don't care, and it doesn't make us somehow inert. Quite the opposite. AIM allows us to engage more resourcefully – to act – or not act – with care, kindness and interest, as seems most appropriate. We can respond creatively to what we find, or we can mindlessly react to whatever shows up.

By developing your AIM you can increase your ability to respond creatively. That can make a powerful difference to your life and the lives of those around you.

Learning to AIM doesn't necessarily mean you'll have more friends, make more money or save the planet – although you never know. But it will make one crucial difference: it will give you more choice. As your ability to choose develops, so you will find that you can begin to act in a more careful and informed way. That will lead to a happier you. In the case of that family gathering, it lets you have a much more productive influence on the people you care about, rather than just putting your head down and losing yourself in watching the drama being acted out around the table – or getting into the script and adding your own unhelpful spin to the reactive dynamic.

In short, you become wiser and kinder.

The important point is that we can all allow and inquire to some extent already. We all have some capacity for meta-awareness. But you can't simply decide to increase these as if that will come about simply because you want it. You've got to *do* things to train your mind to get better at these activities. There are simple exercises you can do to increase your AIM. That is what the Mind Time practices are all about.

This book and the Mind Time practices help you to AIM better. Our confidence in the practices comes from our work over many years, including a three-year study into the effects that the practices had on an individual's ability to AIM by using allowing, inquiry and meta-awareness. The findings were published as a report and a series of articles in the *Harvard Business Review*. (For more about our research see the box below and the section at the end of the book.)

10 MINUTES OF MIND TIME EACH DAY WILL CHANGE YOUR MIND

AIM is a form of mindfulness, which refers to the ability to choose to be aware, in the present moment, of your experience and how it relates to the situation you find yourself in, and to hold that awareness in a compassionate and careful manner. The fundamental building blocks of mindfulness, as we see it, are allowing, inquiry and meta-awareness.

THE 10-MINUTE RULE

The individuals in our research study wished to improve how they performed – as parents, friends and work colleagues. Here are some examples of issues they wanted help with. Which of these resonate with you?

- 'I want to be a better parent and enjoy my time with my children more'
- 'I want to be more resilient – better able to cope with work pressure'
- 'I want to feel like I have more space and time to do other things besides work'
- 'I want to feel less anxious – and just be in a better mood more of the time'

- 'I want to sleep better'
- 'I want to get the most out of my team and help them develop'
- 'I want to be able to deal with my difficult neighbour/ relative/boss better'
- 'I want to be able to be the best friend and relative I can be'

What we discovered was really interesting.

The people who undertook the training showed some improvements in mindfulness and resilience. But the more Mind Time they put in each day, the more significant change occurred across a variety of areas.

As practice times went up, so too did improvements in resilience, collaboration, agility, perspective taking, aspects of empathy and mindfulness. Their levels of personal distress reduced. They reported an increased capacity for self-awareness and self-management, especially around their ability to regulate emotions, see alternative perspectives and 'reframe' potentially difficult or stressful situations both at home and at work.

They also reported enhanced sleep, reduced stress levels and improved work–life balance, as well as increased confidence in the face of difficult situations.

But how much Mind Time was 'enough'? We observed a simple rule at work.

Those people who had done, on average, 10 minutes or more per day over the eight-week period experienced significantly greater improvements in their levels of mindfulness and resilience than those who practised less than that.

Increasing your AIM can change your mind and change your life. Our research, and experience of teaching thousands of people over many years shows that you can increase your AIM by practising some simple techniques. But, as so often in life, the benefits come with practising these techniques on a regular basis. Just like learning a musical instrument, it turns out that changing our minds takes practice. Daily practice. That's good news, because it is achievable. And the even better news is that we know how much time we need to devote to that practice to make a real difference.

On our research programmes we found that with less than 10 minutes a day, there is some change, but not much. But at 10 minutes or more per day, changes really start to kick in. This is an important finding.

Think about it. Just 10 minutes – and you begin to change your mind.

To put this into perspective, let's do the maths.

If you're currently getting the UK average of around 6.8 hours' sleep a day (as opposed to the 7.7 hours on average that most of us think we need), that means you're awake for 17.2 hours each day.[1] That's 1,032 minutes. Ten minutes of Mind Time per day therefore represents less than 1 per cent of your waking hours.

Just under 1 per cent of your time given over to Mind Time and using AIM can significantly improve your life. Moreover, we know from our own experience and from what people tell us, the better you become at working with AIM the more that will improve the lives of those around you too.

Here's another point. The more practice that participants in our research project did, the more they changed. But significant change started at 10 minutes. If they did less, they didn't get much change. So we encourage you to get going and to do *at least* 10 minutes of Mind Time each day. If you can do more, that would be even better. But we found that you're unlikely to get very much benefit if you do less.

The Mind Time practices we taught them allowed our research participants to experience AIM over and over again. So much so, that it began to be habitual. The three aspects of AIM – allowing, inquiry and meta-awareness – became instinctive.

Let's take a closer look now at the three elements, so that we can help you to build them with practice.

ALLOWING

Allowing involves approaching a situation with an attitude of openness and kindness to yourself and others. It's not about being passive or giving up; it is about facing up to what is actually going on in each passing moment and using our energy more productively, rather than wasting it wishing things were other than they are.

Amy is an enthusiastic, but understandably tired, mother of three young children who worked with us for a couple of months to improve her AIM. Absolutely committed to her role as a mother, she wanted to be able to cope with juggling family life with work life, which was also very important to her. She explained allowing like this:

> 'It's that ability to let a few things go more easily, and not worry excessively about them. Take it as what it is. There's also the deeper recognition that there are things you just can't change. Then the best option is to go towards them and be with them.'

Without allowing, our criticism of others and ourselves crushes our ability to inquire and observe what is really happening.

Take the case of Matt, a father who came to us for help. We've known Matt for a few years and although we met him in the context of his work initially, the most important thing for him is his family and how he can be a 'good dad'.

Matt's teenage daughter was getting into trouble at school – and it was getting worse. His levels of anxiety had reached a critical point. Every time she got into trouble, he would fly off the handle. That left him feeling thoroughly ineffective as a dad. He had no idea how to get through to her. He was having trouble sleeping and found himself constantly ruminating over the issue. That began to put his marriage under strain as he and his wife began to blame each other for their daughter's behaviour.

We saw how Matt's situation was affecting his work when we observed him during a team meeting. When he stood up to present an update on how his part of the business was doing, his body language and tone of voice gave away how exhausted and anxious he was. He couldn't meet the eyes of his audience and we saw how he struggled to remember details and answer questions clearly. He stumbled his way through the presentation and left his team awkwardly wondering how to respond.

Talking with Matt afterwards, we asked what had been going through his mind as he stood up to make his presentation.

'I just knew it wouldn't go well. I felt so exhausted, so nervous. There was this voice going on in my head – "You're not going to do well … you're not going to do well …" so I didn't. The more I felt it was going badly, the angrier I got with myself. I told myself, "Pull yourself together!" The more I did that, the angrier I got with myself and the tenser I became. The tenser I got, the angrier I got. I kept thinking, "You're really letting yourself and everyone else down." I guess it's no surprise that I did.'

Things were undeniably tough for Matt and it would have been great if he could somehow have been more open with his colleagues and asked them for help. But that's not always possible in every workplace. What would also have helped, though, would have been if he had been able to hear the voice in his head and react to it with compassion, rather than anger. In Matt's case, though, on hearing the voice he became angrier and, as a result, heaped even more pressure on himself.

Do you recognise this sort of voice? One of the people attending a course we led described it as the *Poison Parrot* that sits on your shoulder – whispering undermining words in your ear.

If he'd been able to see in that moment that the thought 'You're not going to do well' was just a thought, not 'truth'. And then if he could have met that thought with compassion and acceptance – 'Oh yes, there's that thought again. It's just a thought – it's allowed …' – then things might have gone differently. He might have been able to regulate his emotional state a little better. That might have given him the opportunity to breathe just a little bit more, to look up a little more, to settle a bit more, and to begin to inquire into what was going on.

That might have made the difference.

INQUIRY

Now let's look at the second element of AIM.

Richard, a high-flier, is unusually quick thinking and passionate – he can be fun to be around but also breathtakingly energetic. He leads a successful team in a demanding industry. He has a wife and two children, but he doesn't see them much because of work. He wants results and seems to get them. But he struggles with one key issue. He is so quick to react that the people who work for him are scared of him. They're unwilling to open their mouths in case he dismisses their ideas or judges them as incapable. The same is true at home – his wife and kids don't tend to share concerns with him because they think he will offer quick 'solutions' and tell them to just get on with it and stop complaining. Listening and empathising are two things Richard is *not* known for.

Richard is determined to change his behaviour. His marriage and his long-term relationship with his children depend on it. He also believes that for his team at work to function even more effectively, there must be more sharing of ideas, learning from mistakes and more confidence in speaking up.

When we first met Richard, he was aware of his behaviour and the effect it was having but he didn't know how to stop doing it. Teaching him listening skills, or telling him the benefits of collaboration and empathising – things that he was already well aware of – would make no difference. Coercion, persuasion or teaching: in his case they wouldn't change anything.

Instead, what we've been helping Richard do is to become interested in how he's behaving *now*. To focus less on what he is trying to become and, rather, first inquire about how he *is*.

This may sound paradoxical but if you inquire into your *current* experience with interest, rather than trying to be something else, you may naturally respond and change it.

If we ask you, right now, what's your posture like while you read these lines? What position is your spine in at this moment? Which muscles are tight and which are relaxed? While you question and find answers, there's a good chance that you'll subtly change your posture in response. This doesn't come from trying or forcing – or us explaining about good posture and then telling you to do it. It comes from simply noticing. And that noticing doesn't happen unless you inquire in the first place.

The people we have worked with tell us of the key role inquiry played in their path towards being more vital and alive. They learned to take an interest in their own experience.

Jenny is a nurse. She is compassionate and precisely the sort of person you would want to be responsible for your care if you were in hospital. Always wanting to be even better at her job, she practised her AIM with us over several months. She felt that it was her ability to inquire into her present-moment experience that made the most difference to how she dealt with her patients. As she explained:

'I ask myself, "Why am I feeling like this? What's this feeling? What am I sensing?" And I'm interested in it rather than trying to just make it go away.'

Exploring these sorts of questions openly and robustly can be very effective. Simply asking a question and exploring all that follows can lead to change – in and of itself.[2] This might be in an individual's working life or their life outside work. For example, asking someone to consider how and when they speak up well to their boss encourages them to realise how they speak up and how effective their boss is at listening.[3] They might go away from that conversation with a better understanding and a deeper commitment to speak up more. Or they may walk away frustrated, as they begin to see how their boss silences them. That might lead to them applying pressure on their boss to change his or her behaviour in the future. Either way, the system is changed.

Asking questions leads to change.

Inquiry is the ignition key – if we're stimulated to wonder and ask questions, we give ourselves a moment to pause and reflect. If we do not inquire, then we have no impetus to do anything differently or to learn. If we don't learn, we won't change.

META-AWARENESS

When we do Mind Time practices, we deliberately (but gently and kindly) bring attention to our present-moment experience. Then our minds wander. Then we notice that wandering and we bring our focus back to our present-moment experience. In this way, we are exercising the parts of our brain involved in observing and describing experience, as well as those involved in focus and attention. In doing so, we build our capacity to do this to a degree that allows us to call these brain networks into action when we need them most in our daily lives.

This sort of awareness is different to simply having a general sense of understanding. The sort of awareness we are talking about is *meta*-awareness. As we saw earlier, 'meta' means 'beyond' or 'at a higher level'. So we are pointing towards a specific type of awareness. It describes a particular way of *observing* and being able to *describe* what is happening in the ever-changing stream of your experience from moment to moment.

This can be a tricky idea to grasp, although it will become clearer when you actually try out any of the Mind Time practices.

Sometimes the stream of our experience is calm and steady; sometimes it's much more turbulent. We can think of it as made up of four elements – our thoughts, feelings, body sensations and impulses. These combine and recombine in all sorts of unpredictable ways.

The stream of our experience – our thoughts, feelings, body sensations and impulses – is always flowing, always changing, from the day we're born until the day we die. And here's the point: we can be immersed in that stream – just experiencing. Or, at key times, we can notice the stream. We can see what's going on with us. In that moment, meta-awareness occurs and something new and subtly powerful enters the picture.

Meta-awareness enables us to choose.

When we are aware of our thoughts, feelings, body sensations or impulses as *just that* – as just a thought, just a feeling, just a sensation or just an impulse – a new freedom can enter the picture.

We can think of meta-awareness as a wonderful capacity that allows us to do two seemingly contradictory things at once. On the one hand, we're still in the stream of our experience because we can't ever leave that stream. So long as we're alive, we're experiencing. But meta-awareness allows us at one and the same time to step for a moment onto the bank of the stream and to see it flowing by.

With meta-awareness, we're both in the stream and ever so slightly apart from it – objectively observing it, *noticing* what's going on.

Imagine you are on a tall-masted ship – one with big sails and a crew of 50 hard at work on the deck. You hit a storm. You cling on to the side, unable to move. Meta-awareness is the ability to climb up into the crow's nest. You are still on the ship – you are intimately aware of how the lurching of the ship makes you feel; you feel the wind rush at your face – you are very much *in* the experience. But, crucially, you are also ever so slightly distant from it now and able to look down on the rest of the crew, able to see the storm and how it is affecting the ship. You can see the bigger picture.

Peter is a quiet, introverted single father. He took up the Mind Time practices we shared with him partly because he was experiencing quite high levels of anxiety as he tried to manage commitments of work, being a father and also a carer to an elderly parent. For him, it was developing his ability to observe his thoughts rather than be ruled by them that made a crucial difference. He explained:

'The practices gave me a way to take back control over my own thinking. So recognising that I'm choosing my thoughts, and they're not me, they're just the noise of what's going on.'

To get a more immediate experience of what we're talking about, try this experiment.

We'll briefly outline two different scenarios and invite you to reflect on each of them, separately, for a few seconds. If the contents of these scenarios don't work in your own life, when you've read them both maybe take a moment to imagine something that better fits your circumstances.

Scenario 1

You've had a dreadful night. At 3 a.m. you woke suddenly with a low-level feeling of anxiety – and that got you thinking. You know that it's not helpful to pursue thoughts like that at 3 a.m. – they're always somehow exaggerated – but you couldn't help yourself. One thought led to another. To top it off, you then started worrying about the fact that you weren't sleeping and you were going to be tired and significantly below your best for the busy day ahead. So you started to think about that, and that *really* didn't help. Having finally dropped off at 5.30, the alarm woke you at 6.30 and you began your morning bleary-eyed and feeling like there was sand under your eyelids.

That morning, you drop the kids off at school and they leave the car without saying a word to you.

What do you think? How do you feel?

Reflect on that for a few seconds before reading Scenario 2.

Scenario 2

You've had a great night. One of those really comfortable, satisfying nights when you get to bed at a good time, sleep all the way through and wake having had what feels like the perfect amount of sleep. You feel good.

That morning, you drop the kids off at school and they leave the car without saying a word to you.

What do you think? How do you feel?

Now we have just one question for you. Between Scenario 1 and Scenario 2 – was there any difference?

When we talk about these scenarios we usually find that there are a few people who experience no difference between the two. But there will also be a significant number of people who experience the two scenarios very differently.

'In the first scenario I was so irritated,' someone might say. 'I thought, "Oh yeah – that's right, I'm just your taxi service ..." but in the second scenario I experienced that in another way. "Ah well," I thought, "teenagers ...".'

It's exactly the same event – the kids leave the car without speaking – but in one mind state you interpret that one way, in another mind state you have an alternative interpretation.

The way your mind is shaped by the first scenario presents you with a world in which your kids don't care and treat you like a taxi service. In the second scenario, a differently shaped mind presents you with a world where, hey, your kids are just teenagers with their own preoccupations and, while this behaviour is something you'll maybe raise with them another time, for now it's OK. It doesn't necessarily mean they don't care.

What's going on here?

With challenging events we assume that the way we think and feel is caused by that event. 'Of course I feel irritated. Didn't you see how they just walked off without acknowledging me?' But it's not the event that caused us to react in that way.

In one mind-state we think and feel one way about the event ('I'm just your taxi service!'); in another mind-state we think and feel differently ('Ah well – teenagers …'). Not only that. It's also important to see that the way we think and feel about what happens has further impacts on our mind-state. We get irritated when the kids walk off without saying good-bye and that takes our mind-state a notch or two lower. When we're in a more positive and resourceful mind-state, and can smile and let go of it, it doesn't bring us down.

Here's the point. Sometimes we're more resourceful; sometimes we're less. There's no getting away from that. We're not about to say that the answer to all our problems is just to be more resourceful more often. But when you can see this process at work – when you can stand back and be aware of your thoughts, feelings, body sensations and impulses as just that – thoughts, feelings, body sensations and impulses, and not as 'me' or as 'reality' – then you can choose. This is what we call a state of 'intimate detachment'. This isn't the kind of detachment that leaves you feeling some-

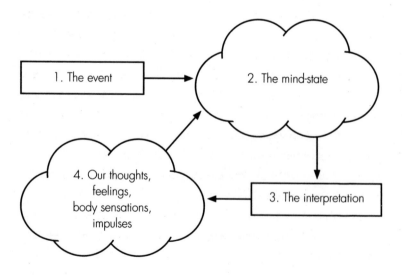

how separate, cold, clinical and not involved in what's going on. Instead, you're close to the experience, intimately involved in what's happening. And at the same time you're able to stand just a tiny, tiny bit back, so you can see what's happening as it happens.

The diagram opposite describes this process.

1. The event – the kids get out of the car at school without saying a word.
2. The mind-state – we're always in one or another state of mind when anything happens. In the example above, if we didn't get much sleep we'd be in one kind of mind-state; if we slept well we'd be in another.
3. The interpretation – depending on our state of mind, we immediately form an interpretation of what just happened. When we're sleep-deprived and struggling with the day we might well interpret that behaviour as fundamentally selfish and uncaring, whereas when we're feeling well rested and more resourceful we might interpret it more as just what adolescents sometimes inadvertently do.
4. Our thoughts, feelings, body sensations, impulses – depending on the interpretation we make, our experience then unfolds in a particular way. A range of thoughts, feelings, body sensations and impulses to act follow from that interpretation. In scenario 1 we might think, 'I'm just a taxi service for them!' That comes with feelings of sadness and a sense of hollowness in the belly and tightness at the jaw. And we might want to cry or go off and get some chocolate. In scenario 2 we might think, 'Uhuh – that's adolescence for you.' That might come along with warm feelings to the kids who are going through puberty; a sense of warmth and openness in the chest area and the resolve to talk about taking others into account when the time is right for that.

Thoughts, feelings, body sensations and impulses. That's one way of exploring the various components of each moment of experience. Meta-awareness is the capacity to observe these in action and realise they are not set in stone; we do not have to succumb to being driven blindly by them.

KEY MESSAGES IN CHAPTER 1

- We spend most of our life on automatic pilot, being swept along by our stream of experiences, habitually deciding on courses of action according to our programmed reactions.
- If, however, we can develop our AIM – allowing, inquiry and meta-awareness – we have more choice in the actions we take.
- Allowing is about meeting our experience with an attitude of care and acceptance, rather than wishing things were different. Inquiry is about being interested in our experience. Meta-awareness is about being able to be both in our experience and, at the same time, just a little separated from it so that we can observe and describe what is going on.
- Our research tells us that we can hone these capacities in a concentrated way through the Mind Time practices.
- The Mind Time practices we will teach you in this book will enable you to choose how you respond more of the time, rather than simply reacting automatically.
- By giving you more choice in your actions, you are more likely to make informed and careful decisions. That is likely to lead to better lives for you, for those around you, and potentially for the environment and society you live in.

The next chapter will introduce you to these practices so you can learn how to AIM.

Chapter 2

Learning to AIM

SHAPING YOUR MIND

We have seen how in one mood we interpret events in one way, while in another mood we interpret them another way. How our minds are shaped from moment to moment determines how we experience things.[1] The Mind Time practices we're sharing will help you first to notice how your mind is currently shaped. And then, over time, like a potter with a wheel shaping clay, you'll begin to discover for yourself how you can reshape your mind. That can significantly change you and it can change the world you experience.

Just as the art of shaping clay is a skilled task that can't be forced, so the art of shaping your mind with Mind Time is also a process that can't be forced. But it can be learned, easily, if you just keep at it for a while.

CHANGE YOUR MIND, CHANGE YOUR BRAIN

In recent years, as brain-scanning technologies have become ever more sophisticated, neuroscientists have come to see just how adaptable the brain is. The way we habitually use our minds, it turns out, actually ends up shaping and reshaping our brains – quite literally. This process is known as neuroplasticity. It accounts for the fact that if people take up an activity such as playing the violin, then the parts of their brains connected with fingering the violin strings show higher levels of activity, even when they're not playing, and in some cases those parts of the brain measurably increase in volume and density.[2]

All the Mind Time practices are forms of mindfulness meditation. And we know that when people engage in mindfulness meditation, over time they too show changes in their patterns of brain activity – and also brain volume and density.

To give just a couple of examples:

- Scientists at Harvard[3] found that people who regularly practised mindfulness meditation over the years had an increased thickness in brain regions related to the ways we sense ourselves as well as the world around us – what we see, smell, taste, touch and so on.
- Another Harvard study[4] found that when people practised mindfulness meditation for just eight weeks they showed changes in brain grey-matter concentration in regions involved in learning and memory processes, the ability to regulate their emotions, their sense of themselves, their capacity to see their own perspective as just one perspective, and their ability to take and try out different perspectives.

There are many more studies like these, some of which we'll refer to as the book unfolds. Scientists are discovering more and more every day about how malleable the brain is and how we can beneficially change it by using our minds differently.

In both of the cases above, the changes that showed up were the result of rather more than the 10 minutes per day of daily practice that we're suggesting as a minimum. Our research tells us that when people meditate for at least 10 minutes a day their experience changes. That changed experience, we believe, will show up in time as changes in brain structure. If you keep using your mind differently, over time you change your brain.

Over the centuries, a vast range of meditation practices has grown up, from many different traditions. There are meditations designed specifically to increase focus and concentration. There are those designed to increase positive attitudes – such as loving-kindness or compassion. There are meditations to increase devotion to saints or gods. There are meditations that are contemplations on the nature of reality, and there are those that focus on sounds such as mantras, or visual patterns or images.

The Mind Time practices we'll be sharing are different to these. Specifically aimed at helping you to develop mindful awareness, practices like them are increasingly being used in clinical, workplace and other secular contexts.

Before we introduce our first Mind Time practice, however, here's a short exercise that will help you experience a key element we'll be working with.

> Take a moment, right now, to look around you. Notice the varieties of white in your environment.
> Perhaps some are tinged with yellow, or with blue, or with grey.
> See how the gradations of white might shift across any one area of whiteness. All the subtle changes.

Now select another colour and do the same.

Now, coming away from the visual, turn your attention to the sound-space you're in.

Pay attention to the varieties of sounds.

To the rhythms of those sounds, the patterns formed by the sounds.

Linger with that for a few moments.

Letting that attention to the sound-space move into the background, now bring your attention to your body and its sensations.

Feel your body in contact with whatever you're sitting or lying on – feel the pattern of sensations there.

Explore that for a few moments.

Now, how are you feeling?

When we teach this we often hear that right after doing this exercise people feel calm, or settled, or more alert.

What's happening is that you're moving your attention from being mainly caught up in mental activity – reading, understanding, thinking, planning and perhaps occasionally worrying – to a much more immediate, sense-based focus. There's an intriguing neuroscience around these two different ways of experiencing, but for now just notice these differences.[5]

Because our minds tend to revert to a thinking/planning/worrying/analysing/daydreaming focus most of the time, scientists call the set of brain networks that deliver these 'the default mode network'. It's what our brains default to when we're not trying actively to do anything else. For example, sitting in a traffic jam with nothing else to do, your mind drifts off into daydreaming, then to worrying about work, then to thinking about your relationship, then to wondering whether to book that family holiday, then back to daydreaming – all in the space of a few short minutes.

During Mind Time we begin to work on that tendency. We learn to recognise the default mode when it kicks in and we learn to choose to come away from it, at least for a time. As you'll see, we do this over and over.

The Mind Time practices we will share are a key to changing your mind. The simple truth is that you will only get the benefits we promised you at the start of this book if you put in the work. But the good news is that it only takes 10 minutes a day. Just 10 minutes to change your mind!

In each chapter, we'll be offering advice and exercises to help you reflect on how these 10-minute practices might help to change your mind and affect your life in key areas.

Our experience, as well as our research, tells us that, as we have said, if you do these practices for 10 minutes or more each day (and the more you do the better), that can help you develop your capacity for allowing, inquiry and meta-awareness. Very broadly speaking, here's how it works:

With each of the different Mind Time practices, we'll invite you to select a different 'focus' – somewhere to place your attention. In the Breathing practice, for example, you'll focus on the breath and the sensations that come along with it; in the Body practice, you'll focus on the sensations you find at different parts of the body in turn, and you'll place your attention on these.

What you'll find is that your attention will stay with your chosen focus for a time and then it will drift off. Maybe you'll start thinking about some of the things you need to do today. Then you'll notice that your attention has drifted away, you'll see where it went to, you'll unhook your attention from where it went, and you'll bring it back to your chosen focus.

And, strange as it may seem, this simple process builds your AIM.

It builds allowing

You intend to keep your attention on the breath but your mind wanders off. You might want to give yourself a hard time about that. 'Why can't I do this simple thing? My mind is so busy! It's so loud in there. Pipe down! Settle! Come on, this isn't rocket science! It's so simple. Why can't I do this?'

You might find yourself carrying on an internal conversation like that. Or, maybe you're doing this in a city where there's lots of noise outside. 'Oh no! Can't I have a few minutes' peace for Mind Time? Car alarms! Again. And that pneumatic drill. Why are they always doing building work?'

Or maybe there's noise from your family. 'Kids! Please ... Just a few minutes ... Please. Where's that husband of mine? Can't he help – just for a few minutes?'

Over and over again, as you listen to the Mind Time guidance, we'll remind you to bring a gentle, kindly, allowing attitude to whatever you find as you sit to meditate.

So you find an allowing attitude for a bit, you settle into it, and then it slips away and another attitude takes over. Then you notice what's happened and you come back to allowing. The allowing slips away again, after a bit you notice what's happened and you come back to allowing. Over and over.

Gradually, you're building your capacity for noticing the quality of your inner state and for choosing to become more allowing. Self-criticism, irritability, harshness, unkindness. We all harbour these to some extent. As you engage in the Mind Time processes you're learning to spot these states more readily – and you're learning to come away from them more easily and to embrace whatever comes your way with a more allowing attitude.

Sometimes it can be fairly easy to adopt an allowing attitude to unhelpful or unwanted thoughts, feelings, body sensations and impulses. At other times it can be very much more difficult.

Experiences like deep grief, loss or shame, for example, can seem at times to be overwhelming and very hard to allow. At such times, though, even the smallest touch of allowing might help to turn down the volume – just a little. If your experience feels overwhelming, approach it with caution. At times it can be like entering a lake of very cold water. You touch your toe in and then withdraw. You approach it again, and then withdraw. Gradually, though, you begin to let yourself down into it a bit further – step by cautious step. There's no rush. Take your time. Eventually, maybe you'll find you can swim.

It builds inquiry

We can think of Mind Time as setting up the dedicated conditions for investigating the complex processes that underlie our moments of experience. To create such conditions, you go somewhere quiet-ish, where you won't be disturbed. That reduces input to some extent. Then, if you're comfortable doing so, close your eyes. That reduces input still further. Sit upright and alert – that lets you pay close attention to whatever you find. Then choose a focus, for instance the breath, and watch what happens.

You will begin to see your inner processes unfolding. The focus on the breath is there as an anchor, to return to over and over. It lends stability and direction to the process. All of your unconscious processes are still running; they don't go away just because you sat down and closed your eyes, only now you can see them.

Over and again, we'll remind you to treat what arises in the changing flow of your experience with a kindly curiosity. Coming back to that, over and over again, builds your capacity for inquiry.

Through inquiring, you'll begin to see where your attention slips to out of habit. Maybe it goes over and again to your to-do list, or to worrying about your relationship. You get interested in that. Curious about it. You see that this is what your attention does now.

This is what's preoccupying you. More than that, you also begin to see and to inquire into what comes along with that. When you're worrying about your relationship, what's happening in your shoulders, in your stomach, in your jaw? Notice any tightening or tensing. Feel it, explore it for a few moments. See what it's like to come away from it. Ease those shoulders, let go of tension in the jaw. Now what's here in your thinking?

In this way, in the dedicated conditions of Mind Time, you gradually build your capacity to notice and inquire into the different, interrelated elements of your experience.

When you become better able to inquire in this way, you become better able to manage and regulate the changing flow of your emotions. You also become more alive to, and curious about, other people and what's happening with them. And you become more alive to the world around you and all the wonderful, infinitely complex systems that your life unfolds in: family systems, social systems and natural systems. As your capacity for inquiry builds so all of these begin to reveal more and more of the extraordinary wonder that you can see unfolding wherever you turn your attention.

It builds meta-awareness

You sit down and select your focus. Maybe the breath. Then your attention wanders and you start to think. You think and think and think – and then you notice that you're thinking. That noticing is a crucial moment of meta-awareness. You're no longer just thinking. Now you're thinking and you're aware that you're thinking. That is meta-awareness. When you have this meta-awareness you can choose what to do next. You let go of the thinking and you shift your attention back to the breath. It's easy to make that move, from thinking to paying attention to the breath, but it's only possible to make it – only possible to choose – when you have that crucial moment of meta-awareness. Meta-awareness is the beginning of choice.

Of course, it's a choice you'll have to enact over and over. You've had 15, 20, 30, 40, 50, 60 – however many years of habit of *not* noticing what your attention is up to. So, of course your attention will slip back into its familiar grooves. But gradually you're now building another habit. The habit of meta-awareness. So now you can see and choose more often where your attention goes.

We've been talking about meta-awareness of thinking, but it's wider than that. With meta-awareness we can also be aware of feeling.

In the example above, if a noise starts up while you're practising and you become irritated with it, you can notice that. You now have meta-awareness of irritation. That can let you choose. You can treat that irritation with kindness and allowing – 'Ah, there are those irritable thoughts again ...' – and you can come away from those thoughts. You don't fight with them, push them down or push them away. Rather, you allow them, perhaps explore them for a few moments and see what they're like and what they are doing to the rest of your system (perhaps they come with particular body sensations, maybe a tightness in the jaw). Treat all that with kindness, and now the overall flavour of your experience is kinder and more allowing.

The alchemists were early medieval 'scientists' who famously set out to change lead and other base metals into gold (in fact they were equally interested in achieving higher states of spirituality and consciousness). What you've done in the process above is another kind of alchemy. Instead of fighting with your irritation you've transformed it into something else.

You can also bring meta-awareness to body sensations. Maybe you notice a little tension in your shoulders, so you move your attention there and explore the sensation. Again, you don't fight it, you don't force anything. Instead you get interested and you explore – with kindness. Placing your attention in that tension, what's there? Do any images come to mind? Any thoughts? That might be a clue. And if nothing comes to mind, that's fine too. Just bring some warmth, some kindness to the tension. Maybe that will soften and ease it. And if it doesn't, as best you can simply allow it to be as it is.

There are also all the rich and delicate sensations that come along with each breath. During Mind Time, you're aware of these and you're aware *that* you're aware of them. That can come with a deep, settled sense of meta-awareness itself.

Finally, there's the possibility of developing meta-awareness of your impulses. For example, you've decided that you want to do a Mind Time practice today but your to-do list keeps invading the practice. You work with it, noticing, allowing, letting go of it – over and over – but after seven minutes you lose your awareness. The list grabs your attention and, before you know it, you've got up and switched on your laptop.

As your meta-awareness develops through the practices, that scenario can play out differently. Your to-do list keeps invading your Mind Time. You keep working with it, gently and kindly return-ing your attention to the breath, and at minute seven you feel the impulse to get up and get on with your working day. But now you notice it. You feel the impulse. And you see it just as that. It's an impulse. Just an impulse. You feel it, allow it, let it pass, and stick with the practice for three more minutes.

In this way, you're developing the unusual skill of seeing impulses for what they really are – just impulses. Most of the time we don't see our impulses in that way. They underlie all our behaviour, but they're mainly invisible to us. There's an impulse – so we act. We see the biscuits sitting on a plate on the kitchen counter and, with-out even noticing our impulse, we take one and eat it.

When, with meta-awareness, you're better able to notice your impulses – and you can see them just as impulses – you get more choice. You see the biscuits, become aware of the impulse, and *you* decide. Do you want to eat one or not? You can choose.

That's great for those of us who are concerned with piling on the calories, but it applies in so many other parts of life. Someone pushes into you in the street; you feel the impulse to say something harsh, but instead you respond more appropriately – and so on.

Allowing, inquiry and meta-awareness – AIM. Gradually, over time, if you can establish the habit of taking Mind Time regularly, your capacity for these builds. Then things will go better for you and for those whose lives you touch. But we also know that it's never easy to establish a regular habit. Before you get going, therefore, there are a few questions you might want to think through.

Finding a good time for Mind Time

When in your day are you most likely to be able to commit to your 10 minutes of Mind Time? See if you can find a time when you won't forget to do it and when you can be fairly sure you won't be disturbed, get distracted or fall asleep.

It's easier to build a habit if you can fit it into a routine. Would it work best for you first thing in the morning – before others are awake? Or perhaps, if you commute into work on a train or a bus, could you use your headphones to listen to audio instructions and do 10 minutes then? Might it work best as soon as you get to work or over a lunch break? Or perhaps when your home is quiet and there is some space in the evening before going to bed?

Finding a place for Mind Time

Choose a place where you won't be disturbed or too distracted by things going on around you when practising. So, if your Mind Time is at home or at work, which room would be most appropriate? Is there a quiet meeting room that could be available at work (not the 'glass goldfish bowl' kind where everyone can see you)? Is there a place at home where others won't disturb you? If you can find a particular space in a particular room which you can designate for your practice, that might help – but don't worry if this is not possible – in the end the main thing is *just do it*.

If you will be practising on the move, don't under any circumstances try to do these practices while driving, but if you're regularly on a bus, train or plane, that might be a good time to set up your routine. A set of noise-cancelling headphones can help, but aren't essential.

Seeking support from others

It can be helpful to have the support of your family, friends and colleagues when you begin Mind Time. Of course, you can't expect them always to support you and we sometimes come across people who found that those closest to them definitely didn't support them – occasionally even teasing them. See if you can find others who will support you. It's helpful to tell a few people what you're trying to do and why, and ask them to encourage, nudge and give you space.

It would be great if you could embark on the habit of Mind Time with someone else. Is there a friend or a colleague who is also interested? You could support and challenge each other to stick to the practice, discuss things when they get tough, and share stories of how your new skills are helping you both. You might even want to get together to practise. During our research, a few people who worked together booked a meeting room and set up a regular lunchtime Mind Time session together. It was one of the main reasons, they said, that they managed to stick with their practice and saw its benefits.

Knowing there is no 'right' way to do this

We often get asked the question: 'Am I doing it right?' Sometimes that's because the person asking has misunderstood what we're trying to achieve in Mind Time. There's a widely held misunderstanding in our culture that in meditation you should somehow be able to get rid of your thoughts or stop your mind from wandering. It's easy to become exasperated when, like almost everyone else, you become aware that your mind is all over the place and keeps wandering.

Our minds wander – that's just what they do. And every time we notice that they've wandered is an opportunity to refocus. Doing this over and over lays down the neural pathways in our brain that help us to be aware and to focus outside meditation. Mind Time isn't about stopping our thinking or feeling. It's about noticing when we've forgotten to be aware and bringing ourselves back to awareness. Sometimes you'll do this hundreds of times in just one session, and that's not a bad thing – it's great practice.

It takes a lot of patience to develop a new skill. If you ride a bike, it's unlikely that you just jumped onto one on day one and pedalled off happily. It's more likely that you fell off several times and got back on several times. That is just how we learn.

Notice what your expectations are regarding Mind Time. We can often expect quick results and continuous progress and that is not always realistic. There will be ups and downs, and change takes time.

So when might I see changes?

As we said, change takes time. We can't exactly predict when and in what form it will occur. Our observation of the thousands of people who have attended courses led by one or other of us is that often they find that the practices give them some immediate relief. For some people, when they start to practise Mind Time, it can help their minds to calm – at least a little. But AIM is very much more than calm. Allowing, Inquiry and Meta-awareness are a set of capacities that emerge from training.

I (Michael) was once approached by a client who wanted me to do some Mind Time work with a group of their employees. But they also wanted those employees to have an outdoor experience. 'Could we combine the Mind Time training with mountain-climbing in Scotland?' they asked. Never one to say no, I thought that would be interesting to try, so I agreed. I wasn't very fit at that point in my life. So I engaged a trainer at my local gym and told him that his task was to ensure that I got up that mountain without embarrassing myself. My task, he told me in turn, was to turn up at the gym three times a week for three months and get on with the training.

In the end, for their own reasons, the client changed their mind and we did the work elsewhere. But I went out with a friend and climbed the mountain anyway. It was great to see how much my fitness had changed in just three months. Just a bit of exercise, three times a week, had changed things considerably.

It's the same with AIM. We build it in the same way we build any other kind of fitness. And just as I'd never have been able to climb that mountain in the first few weeks of my fitness training, so you shouldn't expect the capacities we're discussing here to turn up very quickly. On the courses we lead, we tend to find that around the fifth or sixth week of practice people have come to experience AIM much more readily. But we're all different. Our advice is to start, keep going, and check back in a couple of months.

Here are a few of the things the people we have worked with have said about learning to practise at various times during their journey:

'It's a bit like being a learner driver – you know you haven't got it all completely sorted yet, but you just need to trust yourself to go on the journey and get to that point where you have an established practice with really good tools and really sound judgement.'

'It's just I don't feel I have the time. And every time I have that thought I'm like, "That was the whole point of going on this course!"'

'However hard it felt in the beginning to get into it, it was an incredible place when you got to the end.'

When asked what advice she would give others who were embarking on Mind Time, Sally, an inspirational primary school teacher we know, said:

'It'd probably be something like: "There will be a point where you'll hate it, but if you carry on trying different ways, eventually you'll find something that feels right." Because Michael and Megan had told me early on that at a certain point I might feel like this, I felt all right about it when I did! [Laughs] I think otherwise I would have said, "All right, forget it." But in fact, pretty much everyone in my group was going through the same experience at the same time.'

Expect there to be ups and downs. Take a moment now and again to notice how you may be starting to benefit from your practice. It will take time. But if you commit to your practice, and don't give up, things will start to change. That is what our research and our work with thousands of individuals embarking on Mind Time practice tell us.

Let's move on to the practices. First some general points.

1. Posture and position

You don't need to sit cross-legged on the floor, although you can if you want. It's helpful to be in a comfortable position – but not so comfortable that you fall asleep. Sitting upright in a straight-backed chair is good, and that's what most people on our courses choose to do. If you choose this, get your knees ever so slightly below your hips – that will help lengthen your back. Keep your feet about hip-width apart and pointing forwards if that's comfortable. Feel them making a good contact with the floor. Tuck your chin down slightly; the back of your neck then lengthens.

You could also lie down on a rug on the floor if you feel alert enough when you do that. You can even stay standing – and there are two Mind Time practices we've provided which need you to move or walk. The main thing is that you give yourself every chance to focus on the practice without being unduly distracted by sleepiness or discomfort.

2. Closing my eyes?

You don't have to close your eyes in Mind Time, although it might help you to focus if you do. If closing your eyes is uncomfortable, or leads too easily to sleepiness, just leave them open, lowering your gaze to the floor and letting your focus soften.

3. What to focus on

In each practice we'll suggest a different focus. And we will gently remind you to re-focus, whenever your attention wanders!

In some of the practices we will ask you to move your attention to your breath or parts of your body and keep your attention with the sensations you are experiencing. When we do this we are not asking you to *think* about the breath or your body. We're inviting you to *sense* it – directly. Feeling the sensations that come with each in-breath, the sensations that come with each out-breath. There's nothing you *should* be sensing here, there's just what you *are* sensing. And there's no special way of breathing, no right or wrong way of doing that. All you're doing is allowing your attention to stay, for a time, with the actual experience of breathing as it occurs from moment to moment. Similarly, if we invite you to bring attention to your feet, we are not asking you to think about your feet; we're inviting you to experience the sensations you feel in your feet right at that moment. Again, there is nothing that you should be sensing – it is fine if you don't feel anything at all. We are just asking you to be aware of that.

4. How to stay focused

It is likely during Mind Time that the mind will wander. There's no getting away from that. It's what minds do and it's not a mistake or a fault. But whenever you notice that you've lost your focus, just see where your attention went. It can help to silently say to yourself, 'Oh yes, thinking …', or 'Uhuh – that's planning …', or 'Oh yes – that's me worrying …', and then gently, kindly, return to the focus of attention. It is likely that you will do this over and over and over. And that *is* the practice.

5. How to stay awake

It is extremely common, especially when you start to practise Mind Time, that you fall asleep. Remember that our minds have spent years and years associating closing eyes with sleep, so it is hardly surprising that it is going to take a while to train ourselves that it doesn't always mean that!

Coupled with that, many of us are also genuinely lacking in sleep – some of us acutely so. The American Academy of Sleep

Science says that the minimum number of hours' sleep required for a healthy adult is seven. Many of us get fewer than that, and obviously the quality of our sleep is also vital.[6]

If you fall asleep, don't beat yourself up about it. You probably just need some sleep. If you can, though, find another time that day when you can do Mind Time again. If you keep falling asleep, perhaps you could try doing Mind Time at a different time in your routine when you are likely to be more alert. Or you could keep your eyes open and just lower your gaze and soften it, rather than closing your eyes.

Most of all, though, don't give up!

6. How to transition out of Mind Time

When it's time to end the session, give yourself a little while to adjust. It can take a few moments to reconnect with your day, so don't just jump up and rush into whatever's next on your to-do list – that can be a bit of a jolt to your system. Take your time.

7. Which order do I do the Mind Time practices in?

The simplest and most basic practice is called Breathing. We recommend that you start here. Start doing this every day when you're ready and keep that up for a couple of weeks before moving on to experiment with some of the other meditations we're sharing.

If you want to practise for more than 10 minutes at a time, you can combine practices. For example, some people like to combine the Breathing and the Breath and Body practices. They start with Breathing, and then go on to do Breath and Body.

That's fine. In fact, we recommend it when you feel ready. But for now our suggestion is that you pick one of the practices and stick with it for a while, doing the same practice every day for a week or so, or alternating two practices – perhaps doing Breathing practice one day and the Body practice the next. There's a lot to be said for keeping things simple.

We recommend you try all the Mind Time practices over time and settle with the ones you are most comfortable with, that allow you to settle and to work with your AIM most effectively.

8. Can I do more than 10 minutes?

Definitely! In fact, that would be great.

THE MIND TIME PRACTICES

You can access audio instructions for the practices at http://www.mindtime.me/. You will find that there are two versions of each Mind Time practice (one by each of the authors). You may want to hear a change of voice now and again!

Below is a list of the practices:

1. Breathing
2. The Body
3. Breath and Body
4. Sounds and Thoughts
5. The Present Moment
6. Walking
7. Moving
8. Gratitude
9. Kindness
10. SOS

⏱ BREATHING

This particular practice is a well-known and well-used classic. We recommend you begin here. It's the first track on the downloads. Here's how it goes:

Settling

Give yourself whatever time you need to settle into the posture you're going to use for this practice. There is no rush here and a little time spent settling before you begin to practise can make a real difference to what you find when the more formal practice begins.

Allow your eyes to close if that is comfortable for you. If you prefer, you might leave your eyes open, letting your gaze fall, unfocused, on the floor 4 or 5 feet in front of you.

Setting Your Intention

Take a moment or two to remind yourself of your intentions. This is a time just for you and you're going to use this time as Mind Time – it's not a time to plan or dream or think about a problem. Of course these things might come up. But set the intention now to bring your attention back to the breath whenever you notice that the mind has wandered. And set the intention too to be gentle and kind towards your wandering mind.

Bringing Awareness to the Body

Bring your awareness to the physical sensations in your body right now. Maybe focusing your attention on the sensations of touch, contact and pressure where the body makes contact with the floor and with whatever you are sitting on. Spend a few moments really exploring these sensations.

Focusing on the Sensations of Breathing

When you're ready, shift your awareness to the changing patterns of sensation in the body as the breath moves in and out.

You might let your attention rest with the sensations of slight stretching at the belly with each in-breath, and on the sensations of gentle release there with each out-breath. Or you might find that the breath is more obvious to you from the movement of the ribs or from sensations in the chest or throat or nose.

Wherever you find yourself attending to the breath, see what it's like to rest your attention there for the full duration of the in-breath and the full duration of the out-breath, perhaps noticing the slight pauses between breaths.

There's no need here to try to control the breathing in any way – just let the breath breathe as it does. Even if it seems to be a bit clunky at first, there's no special way you should be breathing. It's simply a matter of gently keeping your attention with the breath – however it is.

As best you can, bring this same attitude of allowing to the rest of your experience – there's nothing to be fixed here, no particular state to be achieved. See what it's like to simply let your experience *be* your experience – without needing it to be anything other than it is.

And When the Mind Wanders ...

Sooner or later (usually sooner), the mind will wander away from the focus on the breath to thoughts, planning and daydreams – whatever ... This is perfectly all right. It's just what minds do: it's not a mistake or a fault.

When you notice that your attention is no longer on the breath, in that moment you're once again aware of your experience. You might briefly acknowledge where the mind has been, perhaps making a very light mental note: 'Ah yes, that was thinking …' and then gently escort your awareness back to the sensations of breathing.

Whenever you notice that the mind has wandered, and it will most likely happen over and over and over again, briefly acknowledge where the mind has been and then gently and kindly bring your attention back to the breath.

Even if you find yourself getting irritated with the practice or with your wandering mind, keep coming back to an attitude of kindliness to your awareness, perhaps seeing the repeated wanderings of the mind as opportunities to bring patience and a gentle curiosity to your experience.

Do This for 10 Minutes

Continue with the practice for 10 minutes or so, perhaps reminding yourself from time to time that the intention here is simply to be aware of your experience in each moment, using the breath as an anchor to gently reconnect with the here and now each time you notice that the attention has wandered.

KEY MESSAGES IN CHAPTER 2

- With just 10 minutes of Mind Time a day we can begin to change our minds. More is even better, but change starts at 10 minutes.
- A big part of the practice is learning to switch from the default network of brain systems involved in always thinking into the experiential network connected more with sensing in each moment.
- Mind Time builds our AIM. You might want to return and take another look at what we said about each of the elements of AIM in this chapter once you've had some experience with the practices. And you might want to keep returning to it over the coming weeks – as your experience deepens, so hopefully what we're saying will speak more directly to what you're experiencing.
- Think about when you'll practise, where you'll do it and who will support you.
- Before you sit down for your first Mind Time session, take a look at our general advice for Mind Time (points 1–8 above). Maybe come back to these from time to time.

Chapter 3

AIM for Better Relationships

In the last chapter we looked at the exercises that, used on a daily basis, can help you change your mind. Hopefully, you have already begun to practise at least one of them. To start with, you may be feeling a little uncomfortable (and even a little foolish) when you do them. You may feel that you're not very good at them or wonder if you are doing them correctly. This is all perfectly normal and part of the journey. By the way, there is no *correct* way to do them, only *your* way, which you will find with practice over time.

It might help to think of it like this. When we first start to learn a musical instrument it can seem a daunting task. It takes time to learn our way round the instrument and to master the basic techniques – knowing where to put our fingers or how to blow to make the sounds we want. We don't expect that to happen overnight. We shouldn't expect to master AIM overnight either. It is the practising that makes the difference. And with just 10 minutes' Mind Time a day, in a few weeks we see the benefits.

> Have you started to practise Mind Time yet? If not, what's holding you back?

Do give it a try – and keep going. Just as with getting more physically fit, it may take a few weeks before you see real change.

In this chapter we look at how AIM can improve our relationships.

OUR RELATIONSHIPS DEFINE US

From a young age, we learn from others how to behave and how to make sense of the world. We describe ourselves in relation to others. Our purpose and efforts in life are often related to others. Many of our feelings and senses are generated through our connections with others – we feel love, sadness, excitement and concern because of our response to, and with, others.

Studies have shown that if we are starved of human contact psychological and physical issues can arise – this is not surprising given the centrality of our relationships. In evolutionary terms, we developed social networks for safety and security. We may not face the same threats any more, but even today we cannot survive without relationships. People with healthy relationships live longer and are healthier. We suffer less from anxiety and depression if we have people around us that we care for and that care for us. In fact, being lonely and feeling you lack close relationships can have an equivalent impact on your health to being a smoker versus being a non-smoker.[1]

While our relationships are as important as they ever have been in our ability to survive and thrive, they're also the reason many of us give for our negative emotions.

When most of us think about issues that might be worrying or upsetting us, our responses are often in part due to relations with others. You might put your anxiety at work down to the relationship you have with your employer, manager or colleagues; your stressful home life to your teenage children; your exhaustion down to having to care for your parents; and your dissatisfaction down to you not being able to afford the nice holiday that your best friend can.

Let's look now at some common relationship issues that AIM can specifically help to address. If we use AIM, it will be better for us and also for those we care about.

COMMON RELATIONSHIP ISSUES

Here's a list of negative feelings that are sadly all too common in most people's relationships – at home, at work, or in the community – but with which AIM can directly help.

Which of these do you recognise from your own relationships?

- **Loneliness** – 'I wish I had closer relationships or more friends'
- **Resentment** – 'I wish they would do things differently – it's their fault'
- **Superiority or inferiority** – 'I wish they were as able as I am/I wish I was as able as they are'
- **Dissatisfaction** – 'I wish this relationship was better/more exciting'
- **Powerlessness** – 'I wish I could influence this relationship more'

Pause for a moment. When you experience each of these feelings what is it like for you? How do you behave when you feel this way?

These feelings can be present in even our most cherished relationships, but we can AIM to transform these emotions. First, though, let's examine each in turn to get a clearer sense of what's going on – for ourselves and for society at large.

Feeling lonely

We all feel lonely sometimes. But 1 in 10 of us feels lonely *often*.[2] Trends in how we work and live can exacerbate these feelings. Work or new relationships can now take us away from where we grew up, and, increasingly, many of us work from home, don't have an office base and feel isolated.[3]

Although the explosion in social media is often blamed for a decline in the closeness of our relationships and an increase in the feelings of loneliness, the jury is still out on this. On the one hand, social media facilitates contact no matter what time or what place we find ourselves in. On the other hand, however, we can experience purely online relationships as low quality.[4]

Of course, one sensible thing to do if we feel lonely is to reach out to others. But there's often a stigma around loneliness that leads many of us to keep such feelings to ourselves. We may be afraid that admitting to feeling lonely means we will be seen as unlikeable, strange or inferior. Loneliness isn't easy to spot because it's not necessarily related to how many friends we have – it's more about how we feel and think inside.

But what that *does* mean is that if we AIM to notice our feelings and thoughts, see and relate to them differently and transform them, we can begin to address our experience of loneliness.

Feeling resentful

We are really good at building up our expectations of others. Sometimes, that seems fair enough. If a client books some work from us, then they can rightly expect us to turn up on time and do a good job. If we ask our family to be a little bit quieter because we have a migraine brewing, then we can reasonably expect them to keep the noise down. And our children in turn can expect us as parents to take care of them.

But life isn't always like that.

One way or another, it is inevitable that others don't meet our expectations – or even agree that our expectations (which we can sometimes feel are indisputably 'right') are reasonable in the first place.

When we persist in thinking that the solution lies in *the other person* changing or apologising, before we know it we find that our state is completely dependent upon another's action. When that happens, our capacity for choice shrinks and we're trapped in resentment. Some of us stay like this for our whole life, unable to escape.

Thankfully, though, in situations like this, AIM reopens choice. We learn to develop compassion for ourselves as well as others. We remind ourselves to inquire rather than stay trapped within unchecked assumptions. We begin to notice the effect of our thoughts, feelings, sensations and impulses in the moment and therefore give ourselves more options to respond productively, rather than react automatically. We learn to appreciate and feel gratitude for those in our lives.

Feeling superior or inferior

Ideally, we'd all have perfect upbringings and we'd feel that we are each as valued and deserving as any other. But that's rarely the case. All of us have unconsciously learned other patterns of thinking and feeling and, unless we become aware of them, they can continue to shape the ways we conduct our relationships, leaving us stuck in uncomfortable patterns we can't seem to get out of.

Alison, a shy and gentle lady we worked with, said that as she was growing up she felt constantly on her guard. Her parents would play the game of being civil towards each other and then suddenly burst into anger, which would often end up being directed towards her, particularly when she was a teenager. She learned that she was in the wrong and to blame for her parents' fights. She learned she was 'not OK'.[5]

Fast-forward 30 years and this pattern of assuming she is to blame still plagues her. When there's any hint of conflict at work, Alison assumes that it's her fault. So she tiptoes round her colleagues and has been told that she needs to be 'more robust and confident' if she wants to progress. She would love to be that – but it isn't that easy. She has a pattern of behaviour that has been ingrained for 40 years.

Such a pattern isn't going to go away with a simple flick of a switch, but she is now seeing signs of hope and change. Using Mind Time over a sustained period Alison is developing her awareness, particularly of her thought patterns.

Feeling dissatisfied

As far as their friends are concerned, Graham and Grace are pretty much the ideal couple. Grace is gregarious, Graham is much quieter, but they just seem to work together. They met when they were both still at school, began a relationship, stuck together through university and have now been married for 18 years. They have two lovely teenagers who are becoming more independent, leaving Graham and Grace to spend more time with each other.

While they were looking forward to doing all sorts of new things together when their children grew up, Graham and Grace are finding it much trickier than they thought they would. They explained to us that over the years they both became 'project managers' for their kids and the household. Everything revolved around 'getting things done'. They did this very proficiently, but they did not spend time nurturing their own relationship and they wound up feeling somewhat dissatisfied with it and distant from one another.

Fortunately, though, they are not blaming each other for that or burying their feelings and concerns. They are determined that their relationship can be enlivening, fulfilling and energetic again, if they invest in it. Since coming on a course and learning, through Mind Time, to AIM, they're now finding that they pause more often to appreciate one another. That is letting them pay attention to all those reasons they fell in love in the first place. They are more able to notice when they slip into interacting with one another on automatic, or when they start taking each other for granted.

Feeling powerless

Whether you are a decorator dealing with a customer who has not paid their bill, a worker who feels they can't refuse the demands of their manager to work at the weekend, or a neighbour who has endured years of stress from the man next door who persists in playing loud music late at night, there are times when we all feel powerless.

The feeling of being powerful or not is influenced by two key things. First, through our life experiences, we have all *learned* and taken on board ideas about our own power. If we were bullied as a child, we might have learned that we are powerless. Alternatively, our parents may have taught us that we could do anything we set our mind to. In that way, the things we learn in childhood shape us as adults.

Then, there are the stories our culture *imposes* about who has and should have power and who doesn't and shouldn't. These greatly affect our perceptions. Racial, sexual, class-based, work-based hierarchy and gendered prejudices, developed by society, can lead us to label ourselves and others in ways that convey status. These are stronger in some contexts and cultures than in others and they can all be reinforced through legal, physical and economic might. We know, for example, how women, even in the developed liberal democracies of the twenty-first century, are still disadvantaged in terms of pay and promotion; or how children from poorer families do less well at school and have reduced expectations; or how young men from Afro-Caribbean backgrounds are underrepresented at the UK's top universities.

When learned powerlessness is combined with imposed power-lessness we can feel that our choices disappear. We can feel that we have no control and no ability, or right, to express our needs.

However, through allowing our experience to be what it is, inquiring more deeply into it and experiencing meta-awareness, we can begin to uncover our assumptions around power and question them. We can notice when our thoughts tell us we have no choice or influence and we can then ask ourselves whether that is really the case. We can choose to show compassion and appreciation towards ourselves, rather than adding to the pressure we are under by telling ourselves that we are in the wrong or that we should be stronger. We find our choices open up again.

TRANSFORMING YOUR RELATIONSHIPS

Negative emotions stick around when we assume that the situation isn't going to change unless the other person does. We might sometimes wish that we could be different, or the other person could be; that we had done something differently, or the other person had. We can come to feel frustrated rather than interested in what is going on, so we stop inquiring. We can also find that we react automatically to the other person, in fixed patterns, and that our emotions rule us – often unconsciously.

We can begin to transform our emotions and alter relational patterns if we AIM to improve our relationships:

- With Allowing, we can become more accepting of, more appreciative and more compassionate towards others and ourselves.

- With Inquiry, we can become interested and curious about the assumptions we make about others – and then check them out.
- With Meta-awareness, we can become better able to spot, in the moment, the signals that we are sending to others, and can choose to respond more skilfully rather than impulsively. And we can notice and then pay more attention to the positive moments in our relationships.

All of this adds up to being able to express our needs to others in a way that they can hear.

How do we do this? The rest of this chapter takes a closer look at these vital skills and gives some information and exercises which, used alongside the Mind Time practices, help to develop AIM.

ALLOWING – BEING MORE COMPASSIONATE AND APPRECIATIVE TOWARDS OTHERS AND OURSELVES

Julia is a bubbly and busy lady who is fun to be around and with a wide array of interests and commitments. She approached us hoping we might help her with some of the issues she faced at work, especially to do with her relationships. After she began Mind Time she described a key change that she had been able to make:

'I talk at a thousand miles an hour, I have an agenda that is thirty points long, and I have been exhausting to be around when we've got a lot to do. I've really made a conscious effort to slow down, and take the time to, not so much just focus on the task, but recognise *there's a person in front of me*, and they're having their own experience.'

Julia laughed as she recounted this – she saw the humour in how she flew around work and family like a whirlwind, never stopping to 'see' the other person. Mind Time enabled her to slow down enough to take note of the other person's needs and to empathise with their situation.

This small change in her behaviour resulted in a huge change in her relationships. Those she worked with felt more seen, heard and understood. They opened up more. Julia was then able to make more informed decisions about how to do things and her colleagues felt more like helping her. She achieved more at work and felt less strained. Her family relationships also began to flourish. For Julia, that all came with an enormous sense of relief.

Julia was directing attention, empathy and kindness towards her colleagues and family instead of seeing them (if she saw them at all) as part of a mechanical transaction. She saw that her colleagues and family members were human beings, with feelings, fears, joys and needs just like hers. She realised how grateful she was for having them in her life, even if sometimes she felt frustrated.

The Kindness practice is one of the Mind Time exercises we did with her and you will see that this is something you can download too. It reminds us how similar other people are to us, thus helping to establish empathy and kindness. If there is a person you find particularly difficult to relate to, or someone you wish to try to understand and care for even more, try using this Kindness practice every day for a week and see how your relationship changes.

Another shorter practice that people also find helpful is the 'Just Like Me' practice below.

⏱ 'JUST LIKE ME' PRACTICE[6]

Call to mind somebody you are having difficulty relating to and/or someone you care about and want to relate to even better.

Then slowly consider each of the following lines, spending at least 10 seconds on each one:

This person has a body and a mind, just like me.

This person has feelings, emotions and thoughts, just like me.

This person has, at some point in his or her life, been sad, disappointed, angry, hurt or confused, just like me.

This person has, in his or her life, experienced physical and emotional pain and suffering, just like me.

This person wishes to be free from pain and suffering, just like me.

This person wishes to be healthy and loved, and to have fulfilling relationships, just like me.

This person wishes to be happy, just like me.

The practice above is done on your own.

There is another practice that you can try when you are in the midst of relating with another person. We call this practice Moments of Kindness.[7]

⏱ MOMENTS OF KINDNESS

Consider a person you wish to be able to care more for, or someone you find difficult to relate to but would like to relate to better.

Next time you encounter them do the following:

- As you listen and speak with this person make eye-contact (assuming this is culturally appropriate). Focus on the fact that the person in front of you is unique and so very human – with all the vulnerabilities, joys and needs that you share.
- Focus on the warmth you feel towards this person. This bit can be tricky if your relationship with them is currently difficult or has been in the past. Nevertheless, focus on something that you *can* appreciate/respect about them, however small, and amplify this feeling.
- Focus on what gift this person gives you – what do you practise/learn/receive from this person? Again, even if your relationship is problematic, it might be that you can acknowledge that this person helps you to figure out what you stand for, or gives you the chance to practise your ability to handle difficult conversations.
- During your conversation, stay present. Be curious as you spot thoughts and feelings coming up for you. Observe these feelings and thoughts rather than be caught up in them, and notice them as simply thoughts and feelings rather than 'truth' and 'reality'.
- After the conversation, note down, on a scale of 1 to 10, how in tune you felt with the person and how much care you felt towards them.
- Set an intention, next time, to see if you can increase that score, and try to do this at least four or five times, reflecting each time on what you are learning and experiencing.

These practices help us to allow for how others are. Developing empathy and compassion for others can increase our happiness and health, as well as theirs.[8]

However, we also need to be compassionate towards ourselves, to learn to take our own needs seriously and express them. Our ability to do this can be particularly important in difficult times.

Take Charlotte, a close friend of ours. Charlotte is someone we admire and respect enormously; she is thoughtful, on the lookout for how she can help others, and always seems to be able to ask the questions that help you to see things in a new and helpful light. Just after she worked with us to learn to AIM, she was diagnosed with breast cancer and endured a year of invasive surgery and rounds of chemotherapy.

She has gone through moments of absolute despair, but she is adamant that her ability to inquire into her own needs, take them seriously and then express those to others whom she knew could and would provide support, has been essential.

She knew that sometimes she just needed people around with whom she felt able to be exactly how she wanted to be – people with whom she wouldn't have to waste energy putting on a show. So there were times when she decided to say no to seeing friends – even when they wanted to help – deciding instead to be with her husband, children and mother only.

She knew when she needed to laugh and when she needed to cry, and which friends were most able to help her with that. She knew when she started to feel overwhelmed with the practicalities of family life, and so she accepted her friends' offers to cook regular meals for her.

When we asked her how important others have been to her, with tears in her eyes she could only say 'pretty darn important', and then she laughed, shook her head and said, 'That is *such* an understatement!' But her ability to notice and take seriously and compassionately her own needs meant she was actually able to meet the needs of those around her who loved her and just wanted her well again.

If we were able to engage with ourselves and each other with the care and kindness shown in Charlotte's story, the impact on all our lives would be immeasurable.

INQUIRING – SPOTTING YOUR ASSUMPTIONS AND CHECKING THEM OUT

The American author and educator Stephen Covey recalled an experience he had one Sunday morning on the subway in New York:[9]

> People were sitting quietly – some reading newspapers, some lost in thought, some resting with their eyes closed. It was a calm, peaceful scene.
>
> Then suddenly, a man and his children entered the subway car. The children were so loud and rambunctious that instantly the whole climate changed.
>
> The man sat down next to me and closed his eyes, apparently oblivious to the situation. The children were yelling back and forth, throwing things, even grabbing people's papers. It was very disturbing. And yet, the man sitting next to me did nothing.
>
> It was difficult not to feel irritated. I could not believe that he could be so insensitive as to let his children run wild like that and do nothing about it, taking no responsibility at all. It was easy to see that everyone else on the subway felt irritated, too. So finally, with what I felt like was unusual patience and restraint, I turned to him and said, 'Sir, your children are really disturbing a lot of people. I wonder if you couldn't control them a little more?'
>
> The man lifted his gaze as if to come to a consciousness of the situation for the first time and said softly, 'Oh, you're

right. I guess I should do something about it. We just came from the hospital where their mother died about an hour ago. I don't know what to think, and I guess they don't know how to handle it either.'

Can you imagine what I felt at that moment? My paradigm shifted. Suddenly I saw things differently, and because I saw differently, I thought differently, I felt differently, I behaved differently. My irritation vanished. I didn't have to worry about controlling my attitude or my behavior; my heart was filled with the man's pain. Feelings of sympathy and compassion flowed freely. 'Your wife just died? Oh I'm so sorry! Can you tell me about it? What can I do to help?' Everything changed in an instant.

We observe others' behaviour and make our own assumptions about what it means all the time. Sometimes that serves us and the other person; sometimes it doesn't.

The picture shown below, describes how we can act upon incorrect assumptions and how, through inquiring, AIM can help us in this process.[10]

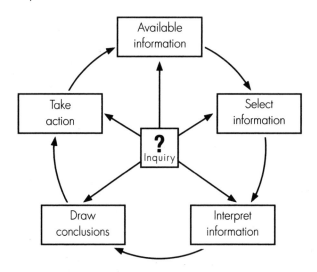

There is a lot of information in the world around us and within us that we could pay attention to, but we necessarily select a fraction of it. We then interpret that information and draw conclusions from it. Those conclusions inform the action we then take, which, in turn, leads to a new situation and the cycle starts over again. At all these stages we have the capacity to inquire. We can ask ourselves whether we are selecting the most relevant information, whether we are applying ill-thought-through assumptions and whether we are drawing conclusions based on very limited understanding. AIM helps us to develop this capacity for inquiry.

In the previous example, the people sitting on the subway selected to pay attention, unsurprisingly, to the children's behaviour. Most of them probably then interpreted this information to mean that the father was doing a poor job of managing his children and concluded that the father was inconsiderate and should take action to control his kids. When Stephen Covey took action and spoke to the father, however, he discovered his assumptions were way off the mark. He then took a different course of action – empathising and asking if he could help.

AIM develops our ability to inquire into our assumptions and, through developing our capacity to observe our thoughts and feelings, spot how we might be choosing, interpreting and acting upon information. We can spot our feelings of irritation and check out what they are based upon. We can observe how our thoughts move quickly towards a conclusion and can pause to inquire into possible alternative interpretations.

Through AIM we allow ourselves the space to choose whether our assumptions are reasonable, and perhaps to make them visible to others and inquire further with interest and compassion.

META-AWARENESS – CHOOSING THE SIGNALS THAT WE SEND

When we meet a stranger it only takes a tenth of a second to form a first impression based on our reading of their facial features. Very quickly, we figure out who is approachable, and who will dominate here.[11] We alter our behaviour accordingly, potentially setting a relationship off on the right or wrong footing. The same sort of reading of signals, with perhaps even greater consequences, happens in our close relationships.

This is where meta-awareness can really help. Our capacity to be aware of the signals we are sending is vital in developing successful and productive relationships. Nancy Klein, an author who examines our ability to listen and think well together, has a great phrase: 'Know your face.'[12] She advises us to develop an awareness of the expression on our faces and what messages it might convey. AIM helps us with this.

Sometimes our face conveys the opposite to what we are actually thinking and feeling. For example, in the workshops we run there can sometimes be someone in the room who immediately draws our attention because they are sitting with arms crossed and a deep frown on their face – then we find out later that this is their 'thinking face' which they wear when interested and deep in thought. We have met others who can't help smiling when they are nervous or when faced with conflict; it is just an automatic reaction that they are often unaware of.

At other times our face and body language might convey *exactly* what we are thinking and feeling. This is great if we are feeling upbeat and positive, but not so great if we are feeling grumpy and stressed. So sometimes we need the capacity to be able to regulate our emotional state and the signals we are sending out, before we affect others. This is where AIM can help.

Our state of mind and body can be 'caught' by others, a bit like a contagious disease. This dynamic is called emotional contagion.[13] When we work ourselves into a threatened state, those around us pick it up. We were trained to do this in evolutionary terms because, if one member of the community froze on seeing danger, it was extremely helpful if everyone around immediately and automatically responded with their own 'threat' mode.

In this way our emotional state spreads like wildfire through a group. This is great if we are all relaxing and feeling connected – for example when we are celebrating with close friends at a wedding. But it's not so great if, when we come home from work and we are stressed and annoyed, we step through the front door and immediately 'infect' all those that we care for.

Have you ever done that? Ever been in a foul mood and come home and noticed that within a couple of minutes everyone's mood has dropped like a stone? Or, alternatively, have you ever come back to a household that is stressed, but because you have had a good day and are feeling upbeat, you are able to cope well and turn things around?

AIM is invaluable in helping us to check in with how we are feeling and thinking and the signals that we are giving to others in the present moment. Only once we notice these can we then choose to change them.

AIMING TO UNDERSTAND AND EXPRESS OUR NEEDS IN A WAY THE OTHER PERSON CAN HEAR

As we have seen in this chapter, we all have needs that we want our relationships to meet. We need to be loved, respected, supported and listened to. These needs lead us to expect certain things of others. Holding these expectations in mind, we look at others' behaviour and make assumptions about what they are thinking and feeling – and whether they are meeting our needs adequately.

If we decide that they are not, we may choose to express our needs to the other person. If we don't AIM – allow, inquire and bring meta-awareness to the situation – then the chances are we may speak up in our default mode, or we may stay silent and bottle up our frustrations.

If we can AIM, however, we have more choice. We can seek to inquire into the other person's experience, and can think more carefully about how to express ourselves in a more informed, caring and considered way. That means the other person is far more likely to listen to us and respond productively.

For example, you might expect your teenage son to stay off his mobile phone and social media just before bed. You know doing so helps his sleep and you want him to do well in his exams (and that makes you feel like a 'good' parent). He, on the other hand, disagrees entirely and believes it is important for him to be online when his friends are, otherwise he misses out on important social interaction.

There is not really a clear right or wrong here – just different perspectives. If we don't seek to articulate our own needs and expectations effectively and try to understand those of others, we can find ourselves disappointed in our relationships and caught in a trap of impulsive reactions.

In this example, it would be easy for you as a parent to lay down the law and, when you catch your son with his phone late at night, assume he is being disobedient and get angry. Or you might half-heartedly lecture him about sleep, eventually giving in, however, and letting him use his phone (which means he is tired the next day). Either way neither you nor your son is learning to take account of different perspectives and thus make more informed choices.

Instead, if you first, calmly and compassionately, inquire into your son's feelings and thoughts, he is more likely to open up. He is more likely to feel respected and to listen to what you have to say. Together, you stand more chance of coming to some sort of compromise.

Using AIM to relate better means we practise how to *both* inquire *and* advocate well. We can trip up by focusing on one more than the other – and sometimes by doing neither!

We can *allow* so that we care for our own needs and so that we feel and express empathy and compassion towards others.

We can *inquire* and become curious about what we need and what we expect and actively ask others what they need and expect in return.

We can develop *meta-awareness* so that we build our capacity to spot our thoughts and feelings, sensations and impulses and can be more careful with the signals we send to others.

In this way we give ourselves choice in our responses rather than opting for automatic reactions, which could be less than helpful. We become far more likely to say something productive.

Being human means being in relationship with others. Our lives are defined through the relationships we have. By AIMing to enhance the nature of our relationships, even just a little, our life can change along with the lives of those we care for.

What's holding you back?

KEY MESSAGES IN CHAPTER 3

- We define ourselves through our relationships. We learn, think, believe, care and feel through relating to others.
- As well as joy, our relationships can bring negative thoughts and emotions, including loneliness, resentment, superiority or inferiority, dissatisfaction and powerlessness.
- To guard against these, we need to become more accepting and more compassionate of others and ourselves. We need to become interested and curious in our experience and the experience of those we are in relationship with. We need to be able to spot, in the moment, what we are thinking and feeling when we relate to others and open up a small window where we can choose our response more thoughtfully.
- Using the Mind Time practices in this book for at least 10 minutes a day – and continuing to do that – will help to develop these three capacities through developing our AIM.

Chapter 4

AIM for Happiness

WINNING THE LOTTERY

I (Megan) always enjoyed spending time with Bess. She had such a warm nature and was always optimistic. She was never bothered by bad news. Financial downturns and political turmoil left her completely unfazed. She was never picky in any way, was always pleased to eat whatever was put in front of her. Possessions meant nothing to her: she wasn't bothered about what she or anyone else wore. And she never needed a drink or a pill to fall asleep – even after a day of excited running around.

Bess was simply contented.

She was a sheepdog, on the farm where I grew up.[1] For humans, it's trickier. We seem to need more.

In this chapter, we'll show you how you can increase your happiness by using the practices we shared in Chapter 2. You'll see how you can begin to use your attention more wisely by engaging in simple activities that allow you to actively build a more stable and enduring sense of happiness and well-being, because you don't need to win the lottery to be happy. In fact, for some people, winning the lottery can be disastrous!

In 2002, Jack Whittaker from West Virginia won the $315 million Powerball lottery jackpot, becoming the world's biggest ever lottery winner. He walked away with $113,386,407 after taxes, enough money by anyone's standards. And Whittaker wasn't poor at the time he won. As president of a construction company, hard work and tenacity had already earned him a net worth of around $17 million.

To begin with, things seemed to go well for Jack. He gave millions to charity and set up the Jack Whittaker Foundation, a non-profit organisation providing food and clothing to low-income families in rural West Virginia.

But it wasn't long before everything started to go downhill. A briefcase with $545,000 in cash and cashier's cheques was taken from his car while it was parked outside a strip club. When asked why he would carry that much money around with him, he simply said 'because I can'.

On another occasion, two employees at the same club were arrested and charged with a plot to drug his drinks with the intention of robbing him. His office and home were broken into and he was arrested twice for drunk-driving.

Then things got catastrophically worse. His granddaughter – on whom he'd lavished love, money and attention – died in 2004. Her body was found, wrapped in a plastic tarpaulin, dumped behind an abandoned van. Cocaine and methadone were found in her system. According to her friends, the cars and cash her grandfather constantly gave her had attracted the attention of some 'bad people', including drug dealers.

'My granddaughter is dead because of the money,' said Whittaker. 'You know, my wife said she wished that she had torn the ticket up. Well, I wish that we had torn the ticket up, too.'

We're not telling this story to make a point about money not being able to buy happiness. In fact, as you'll see, there is some evidence that winning the lottery can make you happier. But not as much as you'd expect.

Rather, the point of this story is that if we want to be happy there are factors apart from money that we really need to attend to. We need to be able to work more skilfully with our own minds. If we want to do that, it helps to have some understanding of the nature of happiness and the positive emotions that give rise to it.

WHERE DOES HAPPINESS COME FROM AND HOW CAN YOU INCREASE IT?

In a famous study published in 1978, researchers asked two very different groups of people about their experience of happiness.[2] They asked recent winners of the Illinois State Lottery; and they asked recent victims of catastrophic accidents, who were now paraplegic or quadriplegic.

They invited both groups to rate the amount of pleasure they got from everyday activities – chatting with a friend, watching television, eating breakfast, laughing at a joke, receiving a compliment, and so on. When they analysed their results, the researchers found that the recent accident victims reported that they got slightly higher levels of happiness from these everyday pleasures than did the lottery winners.

The lottery winners did actually report more overall present happiness than the accident victims. On a scale of 1 to 5, they rated their current happiness on average at 4, while the accident victims came in a fraction below 3. But that was still above the midpoint of the scale. As the researchers said, the accident victims did not appear nearly as unhappy as might have been expected.

Winning the lottery can make you a little happier than someone who has had a recent catastrophe in their lives. But why is the effect so small?

WALKING THE TREADMILL

Partly, it's because of the tendency we all have to get used to the things that once made us happy. Eventually, the thrill of winning the lottery wears off and, as lottery winners get used to the previously unavailable pleasures that are made possible by their new wealth, these are experienced less intensely and so don't contribute very much to their overall happiness.

A friend of ours bought a new sports car a few months ago. For a while, it was very exciting. He'd always dreamed of owning a fast car and the technology had moved on such a lot since the last car he'd bought. Not only was the new car fast, it was also more fuel-efficient than the one it replaced. And it was cleaner and shinier. For a few months, our friend got a small buzz of pleasure every time he got in, and journeys — even on Britain's crowded roads — were more of a pleasure than a chore. But, inevitably, that buzz started to wear off. And now it's just his car again. Nothing special.

Experiences like this point to what psychologists and economists call the hedonic treadmill. Like the more familiar 'hedonism', the word 'hedonic' refers to those things that bring us pleasure. If our happiness depends exclusively on things like the buzz of pleasure we get from buying something new, then we are on a treadmill: we will always be looking for the next hit.

It doesn't work.

Instead, there's another way we can shape our minds.

There's nothing wrong with pleasure. In fact, it's good to seek out, savour and enjoy pleasant experiences. But rather than running mindlessly like a hamster in an exercise wheel, endlessly chasing the next little buzz of pleasure, we can go about seeking happiness more wisely. As we'll see, when we bring Allowing, Inquiry and Meta-awareness into our day-to-day experience, our capacity for enjoyment goes up. We develop a new kind of mind-set — one that is open, interested, curious and kind.

As we've seen, when you do the practices we've described in Chapter 2, you begin to reshape your mind. Over time, Mind Time literally changes our brains, and that changes the way we experience ourselves, others and the world around us. One of the changes that scientists have noticed is that we become slightly more inclined to approach and less inclined to avoid the experiences that come our way.[3]

Why is that?

APPROACH OR AVOID?

A key element in our evolution has been our capacity to reach out for things that will enhance our survival and to avoid things that threaten it. We've learned to approach the things that give us pleasure and a sense of safety and to avoid things that are painful and threatening. This shows up, for example, when scientists measure the degree of electrical activity in a part of the brain known as the prefrontal cortex. The left part of the prefrontal cortex is active when we're in an 'approach mode' – moving towards something with feelings such as openness, interest and curiosity. The right part is active when we're in an 'avoidance mode' – experiencing emotions like fear, disgust, anxiety or aversion.

We all experience some degree of left and some degree of right prefrontal activation as we go through our days. There are things we move towards and things we move away from. But the key issue is which of these two predominates? What is our overall ratio of left/right prefrontal activation?[4]

If our overall experience is more approach-oriented, and our left prefrontal cortex is more active than the right, we'll have higher levels of happiness and well-being. If we're more avoidant, more closed down and anxious – and our right prefrontal cortex is more active – we'll have lower levels of happiness and well-being.[5]

Research tells us that when people engage in practices like those we shared in Chapter 2 on a regular basis, the ratio of left/right activation shifts over time.[6] The practices can help us become more 'approach-oriented' and that makes us happier.

There are two key aspects to this.

First, AIM enables us to adopt a much more resourceful attitude to unwanted experiences. Rather than reacting to what's unwanted, we learn to open ourselves to the experience, and allow it to be as it is. We move towards it with interest and curiosity. And we learn to adopt greater awareness around it, seeing our thoughts, feelings, sensations and impulses as just that – a flow of thoughts, feelings, sensations and impulses. The attitude of 'intimate detachment' we discussed in Chapter 1 is hugely helpful when things don't go as we want them to. (We'll discuss this in much more detail in Chapter 8, which explores how we respond to unexpected and often unwanted events.)

Second, AIM enables us to get much more from the positive experiences that come our way. We notice them, take time for them, value them and savour them. And that's important because our default position is not to pay them too much attention. This is because we're wired for negativity.

Have you found a good place for Mind Time yet?

If not, do keep experimenting. It can take time to figure that out.

WIRED FOR NEGATIVITY

The way evolution has shaped our brains means that they're like Velcro when we have negative experiences, and like Teflon for positive ones.[7] Negative experiences tend to stick with us, while positive ones tend to slide away. Scientists call this our 'negativity bias'.[8] It seems that even when they're equally intense, events that are more negative in nature – unpleasant thoughts, emotions or social interactions; harmful or traumatic occurrences – have a greater effect on our psychological state and processes than do neutral or positive events. In other words, positive experiences generally have less of an impact on the way we think, feel and experience than something equally emotional but negative.

It's easy to see why evolution shaped us like this. If you miss out on a possible positive experience – the chance to mate or get some food – there will likely be another opportunity for that soon. But if you miss out on a potentially negative experience, such as not noticing the presence of a predator, that could well be your last ever chance to do anything. The trouble is, even though most of us now live in a much less predatory environment, evolution hasn't caught up with that and we're still wired to emphasise the negative.

At the business school where we work we sometimes run programmes together. Afterwards, participants are asked to rate various elements of the programme on a scale of 1 to 10 and to add comments if they wish. We read these avidly, looking for ways to improve our teaching, trying to see what worked and what didn't. And it's always somewhat ironic to see how our own negativity biases play out in the process. We can read 15 feedback sheets that rate us 9 or 10. They're full of grateful, appreciative comments. But if the 16th sheet rates us at 7 or below, and if there are any sceptical or even slightly critical comments on it, then our attention is immediately hooked. All the good things people said fall away, sliding effortlessly from our Teflon-coated positivity receptors as the Velcro-like negativity receptors hook remorselessly onto the single negative comment.

We will exchange wry smiles, seeing how our negativity bias is playing out in that moment. This doesn't mean we don't give critical comments their due attention. We do. But we also need to consciously remind ourselves about the more positive comments we received. It takes this small degree of conscious effort to get things into perspective.

Do you recognise this in your own life at work or at home? How often do you focus in on the negative and ignore the positive? It's part of the human condition and we need to give negative comments their due; however, it is important not to ignore the positive.

NEGATIVE–POSITIVE: CHANGING THE MIX

It doesn't take much to compensate for the negativity bias. The bias is instinctive and unconscious, and when you know about it you can make conscious choices that incline your experience towards higher levels of happiness and well-being.

The practices we've shared in Chapter 2 will help you to manage your own reactions better. If you want to truly flourish, there's more you can add into the mix. As well as toning down your reactions to negative experiences, you can actively cultivate positive ones.

Each of us has what some scientists call our own 'positivity ratio'.[9] This is the ratio of positive to negative emotions that we experience over the course of a day. Although researchers aren't agreed about the precise numbers involved in the ratio, it's thought that even people whom researchers describe as 'languishing' – which is several steps up from being depressed or clinically anxious – generally experience *more* positive than negative experiences during a typical day.[10] The trouble is, because of the negativity bias, positive experiences often slide away unnoticed.

If we want to go beyond languishing to flourishing, we need to up the stakes still further. To overcome our negativity bias we need to actively seek out positive experiences. To compensate for the negativity bias we don't only need *more* positive experiences, we also need to consciously take a few moments to savour and enjoy the ones that we do experience.

As an example, in the retail park in my (Michael's) home town recently, I noticed the scent of lime trees in full bloom. That immediately transformed my sense of an otherwise rather bleak and sterile environment.

BECOMING MORE POSITIVE

If you savour them, even quite small positive experiences change your overall experience. But what do we mean by positive experiences? And what's involved in savouring?

Professor Barbara Fredrickson is one of the world's leading experts on the science of positive emotions. Her research led her to identify 10 basic positive emotions: joy, gratitude, interest, serenity, hope, pride, amusement, inspiration, awe and love.[11] Although there are other sorts of positive emotions, of course, these are the ones that colour people's lives the most. Seeking these out and savouring them will leave you feeling happier. And in case you're now thinking, 'That's all well and good, but isn't this a bit self-indulgent? A bit selfish?', here are a few facts from a variety of studies that might help to set your mind at rest:

- **Positivity changes our relationship with others – rather than being selfish, positivity enables us to feel closer to others.** Researchers divided volunteers into three groups and asked them all to rate how close they felt to their best friend. After that, individuals from one group were shown film clips of a comedy routine; another group saw a clip from a horror movie; and a third group watched an instructional video.

Having thus been 'infected' with positive, negative or neutral feelings, they were asked to rate how they felt about their friends a second time. Those who were more positive now (after watching the comedy) tended to think of themselves as being closer to their friends. Rather than being selfish, positivity enables us to feel closer to others.[12]

- **Positivity reduces prejudice – it helps to offset things such as our inherent racial biases.** The familiar racist slur 'they all look the same to me' has some grounding in fact. But it turns out that this tendency can be offset, and even overcome, by increased positivity. Under the influence of positivity people became just as good at recognising the features of people of a race different to their own as they were to those of their own race.[13]

- **Positivity enhances creativity.** Using different kinds of music, a team of scientists infected volunteers with positive, negative or neutral moods.[14] Among other things, they then asked the volunteers to come up with a word that linked three other given words; for instance, 'mower', 'atomic' and 'foreign'. The linking word here would be 'power'. The more positive the volunteers were, the more creative they were with the task.

- **Positivity helps us deal with adversity.** Researchers surveyed a large group of university students, measuring their levels of positivity as well as their tendencies to handle stresses in an open-minded way. They did this by posing various questions, which were variants on the theme of 'When you face problems, do you step back and envisage a wide range of possible solutions?'[15] The more positive people were, the better they were able to manage adversity in an open-minded way, seeing a wider range of solutions. And when the researchers returned five weeks later to survey the students a second time, they found that those who had been more positive at first were even more positive the second time round. The openness they had shown had allowed them to find solutions to the problems they faced, further strengthening their positivity.

- **Positivity feels good.** That's important, and not in a self-indulgent way. Feeling good increases our sense of being competent. It enhances the sense that our life has meaning and purpose. It increases our overall optimism, resilience and self-acceptance. Feeling good enables more positive relationships and it improves our physical health. Feeling good helps us to build the enduring personal resources we need to navigate our life's journey more successfully.[16]

We can all become more positive.

Here's how:

SEEKING AND SAVOURING POSITIVE EXPERIENCES

As we've seen, AIM helps us to become less reactive. It helps us to respond more and react less when things don't go as we want them to. But it's not just that AIM helps us to be more resourceful at times of difficulty. It also – and perhaps more significantly – helps us to notice, explore and enjoy more of the good things that come our way. And that's important. As we've seen, we're wired not to notice positive states very much. But when we're more aware, allowing and curious, we're more likely to notice and consciously enjoy the good things that would otherwise slide away unnoticed.

Ashridge House, where we both work, is a beautiful and ancient former stately home, set in hundreds of acres of parkland and formal gardens. There are rolling views of the green English countryside all around. On some days, it takes your breath away.

The staff car park is set apart from all the beauty, down an incline where it won't spoil the view. When I (Megan) first started working at Ashridge, I used to park, pull out my phone and walk briskly across the main lawn to my office – checking my emails and diary. Then one day I realised what I was doing. What an extraordinary waste!

Let's look at what happened in that moment of noticing.

- Meta-awareness kicked in. I noticed what I was doing.
- Allowing that, I didn't get into telling myself off. I didn't create any unnecessary drama around that. I just smiled to myself – seeing how my habits were playing out – and I resolved to begin to lay down a new and more resourceful habit.
- Inquiry engaged. I looked with real interest at my own habitual behaviour. And I looked with interest at the beauty I was ignoring – the shape of the trees, the colour of the sky, the line of the buildings …

Once AIM had engaged, my experience of that walk wasn't the same again. That momentary pause, when I saw what I was doing, opened a space where I realised that here was an experience I could really savour.

Since then I've kept my phone firmly in my pocket and I take the three minutes' walk as an opportunity to savour – to drink in the extraordinary beauty all around me that can lift my heart and set me up for a productive day ahead.

Those first few moments of noticing my old habit, and the new habit of noticing and savouring the beauty all around me, make a real difference to the course of my day.

We don't all work in such glorious surroundings. But every day brings many opportunities to notice and to take a few moments to savour the positive experiences in our everyday lives.

It's worth taking a few moments to reflect on the ten different positive emotions we mentioned earlier. For a start, it's good to notice the variety. There are so many different ways of experiencing positivity. By taking a little time now to reflect on these and feel what they're like in your own experience – how you feel them in your body, for example – and to sense what each one of them uniquely contributes to your overall mood, you can begin to develop the skill of noticing and valuing them when they come to you in daily life.

Remember, our brains are like Teflon for these positive emotions. We experience them and then forget them so quickly. But AIM can help us to spend more time with them when they spark up in our day. Noticing, and taking a bit of time to savour and enjoy each one when they occur, can begin to change the shape of our day.

We don't need to win the lottery to be happier. Sometimes, all we need to do is to notice and appreciate the moments of happiness that are already there.

Joy

Think of a time when you felt joy. There's a wonderfully unexpected quality to the experience. Each moment of joy is unique. There are the feelings of delight that come from being with those you love and whose company you enjoy. The feelings of uplift, release and appreciation that come from being at ease in nature and seeing something that delights. Receiving an unexpected present or being given a compliment – all of these can be entrances to moments of joy. Joy tunes up your senses; the colours seem brighter, your face lights up and you feel a kind of inner glow.

I (Michael) have four grandchildren. Time spent with any of my grandchildren is a pretty sure way of experiencing moments of joy. Ollie is just over three years old and he loves to run. 'Go faster, grandpa, let's go faster. On your marks, get set, GO!' and off we run. For me, it's not only Ollie's utter joy and delight in such moments that's infectious – it's also the smiles of the other pedestrians coming towards us. Seeing this little boy laughing and bubbling with joy, seeing me holding his hand and running, grinning from ear to breathless ear, they smile and laugh along and little ripples of delight spread out across the parks of Cambridge.

Take a moment to reflect on what brings you joy. What works in your life? How might you arrange things so that you have more joyful moments?

Gratitude

Gratitude opens our hearts and feeds our impulses to give back. Take a moment to think of the things you're grateful for: any of the caregivers, mentors or teachers that have nourished you. The complex network of services and all the servers who make our modern lives work – the refuse collectors, electricians, plumbers, bank workers, street fixers, firefighters, police, doctors and nurses. Each of these is often willing to do a little more than their contracts of employment specify so that life will be smoother for others. Think of the ways you benefit from the combined goodwill of so many invisible others. Think of the air you breathe, the nourishing food you eat, the clean water that flows on command, and all of the effort that's been invested by countless others to make this possible.

Think of five things you are grateful for – right now. Anything will do, big or small. Just five things.

Savour that feeling of gratitude. Stay with it for a few moments.

Research suggests that if we spend time once a week noting five things we feel grateful for, large or small, it can increase our overall level of happiness.[17] Just once a week will do. The researchers found that people who were asked to do this three times a week over the same period didn't experience the same benefit – perhaps because they got bored with the practice.

Serenity

Serenity shows up when our surroundings feel safe and familiar and we don't need to be putting out much effort. It's that feeling of ease and comfort that may come when we're lying in bed at the weekend in the moments before we rouse ourselves to engage with the day. When we're just content to be there, at ease, needing nothing, feeling what we feel, leaving our thoughts to drift. It's the feeling of settling in at home with a warm drink – alone or with a quiet companion – enjoying the comfort of the chair, the ease of being home. It's the feeling of being out in the country or by the sea with nothing needed of us, nothing to do – a feeling of just being.

Can you connect with feelings of serenity right now? What was it like last time you felt it? Next time you notice it, perhaps choose to consciously linger with it for a few moments. 'Ah yes – this is serenity. How good to feel it!'

Interest

Serenity involves letting go of effort. Interest is more active. Something sparks and catches our attention and we're moved to engage and explore. We want to go further down that track, read deeper into that book, explore further on the internet or follow a set of challenges that will let us build new skills. When we're interested, we feel open and alive, we sense our horizons expanding as possibilities open up around us.

When was the last time interest drew you in? What did that feel like? And what might interest you today? Can you find a few moments to pursue an interest today?

Hope

When everything is going our way there's little need for hope. Unlike the other positive emotions, it finds its place when things aren't going so well or when there's a lot of uncertainty about how they'll turn out. Hope especially comes into play when we've lost our job or when someone close to us gets ill. It's a kind of 'fearing for the worst but hoping for better'. Deep within it there is a core belief that things can change for the better. When things are going badly, hope can sustain us and keep us going.

Hope also has a part to play in more everyday matters. We have hopes for today, hopes for this week, maybe. As the authors, we have hopes for this book – that it will be useful and help people.

Take a moment. How is hope playing out in your own life right now?

Pride

Unhealthy pride has two ugly cousins – shame and guilt. These can overcome us when we feel we've done something bad. And it's a sad fact of life in some parts of the Western world that irrational shame and guilt can plague some of us. Some of us feel guilty about our sexuality, for example, or are ashamed of our body shape. AIM can help with troubles like these. We can see more clearly what's behind these feelings, notice how they affect our behaviour and, with a greater kindness towards ourselves, we can let what is the case be the case more easily.

But a healthy pride, which isn't the same as the over-inflated sense of ourselves that goes by the same name, is much more helpful than these.

Positive pride comes when we have done something good that we're happy to take credit for. When it is tempered with humility, it is the good feeling you get when you've achieved something you set your mind to. 'I finally managed to change the washer on that dripping tap.' 'I achieved that target.' 'I overcame my fear of public speaking.' 'I learned to play the guitar.' Pride is especially resonant when we do things we know will be appreciated and valued by others.

Pride is a great motivator. There is good research evidence that when we feel pride we're much more likely to keep going with difficult tasks. [18]

What makes you feel proud right now? How does your body respond when you experience feelings of pride?

Amusement

Sitting round the dining-room table, my (Megan's) two daughters, Mia and Lottie, were discussing whether they looked most like me or their dad. Lottie concluded that she looked most like me and there was broad agreement around the table. When I pointed out to Lottie that I didn't share her dimples, she looked concerned. Leaning forward and tracing her little finger gently along the many fine lines around my eyes, she said: 'Oh but Mummy you have LOTS of dimples – they are just a different shape to mine – they're longer.'

Children are a never-ending source of amusement, and my husband, Steve, and I decided early on to keep a book to record the little instances that made us laugh so much – understanding that these stories often slip from memory all too easily. We occasionally look back at the book and share the laughter all over again with Mia and Lottie.

Sometimes we laugh alone, and that can lift our mood, but when we share amusement with others, the benefits to our mood are very much greater. Like yawns, laughter is highly contagious. Although there is such a thing as cruel laughter, one of the important social signals of shared laughter is that this space is safe. When we share a laugh with someone, it's a signal that we feel at ease and that we're ready to connect.

When was the last time you really laughed with other people? How did that affect your mood?

Inspiration

'Be inspired' is the motto chosen by Sport England and UK Sport to increase participation in sport following the record-breaking success of the British Olympic and Paralympic teams. For weeks during the London and then the Rio Olympics, the news, headlines and television coverage were dedicated to the extraordinary spectacle of sporting heroes pushing themselves to the limits of their endurance. Seeing human nature at its best – whether in sports, the arts or social activism – lifts us out of the confines of our own narrow self-concern.

It's inspiring to observe the great titans of sport or the arts, of course, but there's also the inspiration that comes from seeing someone who is clearly nervous push through those nerves and give a great speech at a wedding, or seeing a busy doctor in a hospital take the time to guide an elderly visitor through the maze of wards and corridors. Inspiration infects us with a sense of what human beings can do. It lifts our spirits and opens new possibilities in our own lives.

The wicked sisters of inspiration are resentment and envy, and it's worth taking a few moments to reflect on the difference between the closed-heartedness of these two and the open-heartedness of inspiration. We can spiral upwards or downwards – the choice is ours.

Take a few moments now and think about who inspires you. What is it about them that's so inspiring? How do you feel when you think about them?

Awe

Like inspiration, awe is a self-transcending emotion. It takes us out of ourselves, jolts us out of the familiar ruts of our thinking, feeling, sensing and acting and opens new possibilities of experience. Awe instantly broadens our horizons: a great cathedral, a stunning sunset, a mountain landscape. We just stop and stare, humbled.

The self-transcending nature of awe means that there's often a small whiff of danger that comes along with it, a hint that our familiar sense of ourselves may be under threat as awe changes our perspectives.

For me (Michael), the fifteenth-century interior of King's College Chapel in Cambridge is a reliable source of awe. As grand as any cathedral, its exquisitely ornamented vaulted stone ceiling soars above vividly coloured stained-glass windows. Standing, looking up, taking a few moments to allow the intricate harmonies of the architecture to work their magic, I often come away from a visit feeling that my eyes have been cleaned and my heart opened.

Love

Love comes last in this list because it needs to have its full due. It's the supreme human emotion. But when we speak of it here we're not referring only to certain specific sub-categories of love, such as romantic love, or the love we have for our children and close members of our family or good friends. Nor are we talking about the excited feelings of desire for intimacy that come when we fall in love. Rather, we're speaking much more broadly, about the experience of a deeply felt wish that others thrive. When we love someone, anyone, we want them to do well. Call to mind someone you think of as a loving person. Our bet is that one of their primary characteristics is that they show a warm goodwill towards others in general.

In one experiment, Professor Fredrickson and her co-researchers recruited a group of 139 adults.[19] Half of them were taught a loving-kindness meditation that involved directing their emotions towards warm and tender feelings in an open-hearted way – a similar meditation to the Kindness practice we have shared (see pages 63–6). The other volunteers were a control group. They learned the meditations later, but before they did, they were available to test against the experiment group to see if the meditations made any difference.

The participants were first asked to focus attention on their heart region and call to mind a person for whom they already felt warm and tender feelings – a child, or a close loved one. They were then asked to extend these warm feelings, first to themselves and then to an ever-widening circle of others.

The participants practised less than an hour a week. Compared to the control group, the meditators reported increases in all of the ten positive emotions.

• •

We can use our minds to change our overall level of positivity. In doing that, we can become happier – of course – but so much else changes as well: our social relations, our levels of prejudice and creativity, even our ability to think more clearly.

NOURISH YOURSELF

Here's an exercise you might try that can help you to tweak your daily routine to increase the amount of positivity you experience each day.

On a piece of paper, list all of the things you do in any typical day. Keep it simple and use broad brush-strokes.

If I (Michael) were to do this, I'd go:

Wake up.
Go downstairs and get a cup of tea.
Feed the cat.
Chat with Annette (my wife).
Walk to my garden studio for Mind Time.
Walk back to the house.
Breakfast with Annette.
Walk back to the studio to work.
Email.
Make calls.
Head off to see a client.
And so on …

Now, take a look at your list and categorise each of the activities you've put down. Put a (+) next to the activities that nourish you, a (-) next to those that deplete you, and a (/) next to those that are neutral.

   Michael's list would now look like this:

Wake up. (/)
Go downstairs and get a cup of tea. (+)
Feed the cat. (-)
Chat with Annette. (+)
Walk to my garden studio (+)
Mind Time. (+)
Walk back to the house. (+)
Breakfast with Annette. (+)
Walk back to the studio. (+)
Email. (-)
Make calls. (+, or –, or /)
Head off to see a client. (+)
And so on …

Now, think carefully. Are there any items marked (-) on the list which you might be able to change to a (/) or even a (+) by doing them differently? Is there any way you might change a (/) to a (+)? Is it possible to spend more time with the (+) and less with the (-)?

Even small tweaks can add up to significant differences. When I (Michael) did this exercise once with a class, one of the students was surprised when I marked my walk to my garden studio as (/).

'But you're walking through a *garden*, Michael. How can that ever be neutral?'

And she was right. Ever since then I've taken just a few moments, when I remember, to pause and savour that. I look around and see what's coming into bloom or dying back. I take in the colours and scents. It makes a small but significant difference to the way my day begins.

With AIM, we can increase our happiness.

Recognising that, like all of us, evolution has wired our brains for negativity, we can begin to see when our attention has got stuck more with what's currently wrong in our experience than with what's right.

When we find ourselves hooked into a negative state, the allowing part of AIM helps us not to judge ourselves harshly for that. Not to beat ourselves up. Instead, we can notice, allow, and bring a bit of kindness to ourselves in the moment.

Then, the inquiry aspect of AIM helps us to look more deeply into that. What's going on in our thoughts, feelings, sensations or impulses that's giving rise to this negativity right now? Can we explore that for a few moments?

The meta-awareness aspect of AIM helps us to see that wherever our attention has been hooked, the thoughts, feelings, sensations and impulses that come with that are just thoughts, just feelings, just sensations, just impulses. They're not 'us', nor are they the final description of how things are. After all, we know that we can think differently, feel differently.

Allowing what's here right now, inquiring into our experience, aware that these are just thoughts, just feelings and so on, we can begin to find another orientation to what's going on.

As we become more accepting of what we find, maybe our attention can begin to slip from the Velcro hook of negativity. Is there anything more positive here right now? Turning towards that, savouring it for a few moments, we can use even tiny moments of positivity to change our overall experience.

What time of day best suits you for Mind Time?

If you don't know that yet, do keep experimenting.
What's it like to do it first thing in the morning? How is it when you do it last thing at night?

KEY MESSAGES IN CHAPTER 4

- The hedonic treadmill means that we're really bad at figuring out what will make us happy. We think that getting something or having a particular experience will make us happy, but we get that thing, have the experience, get used to it, and it stops making us happy. That can leave us like a hamster on a wheel, chasing after happiness.
- Developing an 'approach orientation' – moving towards experiences, even those we don't want, with kindness and curiosity – helps us to become happier. AIM can help with this.
- Evolution has wired our brains so that they're like Velcro for negative experiences, and like Teflon for positive ones. That means we have a 'negativity bias'.
- We can begin to compensate for our negativity bias by seeking out and savouring positive experiences, such as love, joy, gratitude, serenity, interest, hope, pride, amusement, inspiration and awe.

Chapter 5

AIM for Effective Work

We've already seen how AIM can make a difference in our relationships and overall sense of happiness. Hopefully you are practising the exercises from Chapter 2 and are already seeing some benefits from just 10 minutes' Mind Time each day. As we will see in this chapter, AIM can also make a big difference in our working lives.

Can a friend, a family member or a colleague support you in establishing the habit of Mind Time?

Perhaps try asking someone.

THE WORKPLACE REALITY

Ashridge Executive Education, where we both work, sees thousands of people come through its doors every year to learn how to manage and lead in their workplaces more effectively.

Let us introduce you to two people we met recently, whose stories are similar to many we hear.

Linda is an executive at a well-known chain of coffee shops. Normally lively and optimistic, she comes across as having things at work pretty much under control. But her company has been restructuring, trying to reduce costs, and that has thrown things into turmoil.

We caught up with her recently. She was shattered and demoralised, not having taken a proper break in nearly a year – which was when we had last seen her.

The word that popped up time and time again was 'busy'. There was just so much to do. Colleagues had been made redundant; team members who had left had not been replaced. And yet expectations in terms of results had not gone down – far from it; Linda and her colleagues were expected to achieve even more than before. Workdays were longer and longer. Meetings were rife – and back-to-back. Emails were unmanageable: 200 a day with no time to respond.

While previously Linda had been an enthusiast for learning and improving the way things were done at work, she now rolled her eyes at the word 'change'. It no longer had any meaning because it felt like at work they were *permanently* in a state of change. There was no respite. Just a relentless drive to do things differently.

Things felt out of control. She felt she was permanently playing catch-up, but never actually progressing things to meet the expectations of her manager. A cold had lingered for weeks but, she said, 'I just don't have time to be ill!'

She had a haunting sense of insecurity – would she be next in line for redundancy? But despite this uneasiness, Linda felt she had to appear to be in control and confident – someone who could 'stand the heat' and inspire her colleagues, not to mention her customers, in difficult times. But she often felt like she wasn't up to it. Increasingly being given more and more responsibility with fewer and fewer resources, she thought that any moment her colleagues and her boss would start to see the cracks emerging and discover that she wasn't as capable as they seemed to think she was.

That thought wasn't helping.

Pretending she was confident was taking up a lot of energy, and energy was a really scarce resource at that point. Linda felt she was running on empty.

Robert is someone else who was struggling at work. Mild-mannered and friendly, Robert had a different issue. He was a mid-level manager at a manufacturing company in Germany. He had been at his organisation for 15 years and found work 'OK'. He had been promoted relatively quickly but he was bored. He found what he did predictable and lacking in meaning. He felt under-challenged. Like Linda, he felt the need to keep up appearances, although for him this meant portraying an enthusiasm which he didn't really have. Although he was apathetic about what he did at work, he didn't want to lose that job – for one thing, he didn't really know what else he would do – and he was the family breadwinner.

Despite painting this rather bleak picture, both Linda and Robert told us that there *were* aspects of work they enjoyed. They both generally liked their colleagues. Linda recognised she was getting amazing experience that would boost her CV in time, and Robert, while feeling he could up the pace a bit, appreciated the flexibility in his job that allowed him a reasonable work–life balance so that he could spend time with his kids.

Their shared questions were whether they could somehow come to enjoy things more and feel that they were performing more effectively.

By helping us to step out of automatic pilot – by assisting us to be responsive rather than reactionary – AIM relieves three key work pressures raised in our conversations with Linda and Robert. These three, from our experience, are very widely shared.

AIM helps us to move from:

- being automatically busy, busy, busy, towards responding better to workload pressures;
- finding ourselves passively on the receiving end of change, towards feeling more aware, at ease and proactive; and
- feeling trapped in the need to keep up appearances, towards being more compassionate and authentic.

We will see, in each case, how shaping your mind to be more allowing and inquiring and to develop meta-awareness can help you to thrive at work rather than simply survive.

BEING BUSY, BUSY, BUSY

How often do you ask a friend how they are and they say: 'Busy – just so busy!'

Do you often respond like that too?

Many of us feel under increasing time-pressure. More and more of us are holding down multiple jobs.[1,2] If you're an average desk-worker today, you're currently receiving over 120 emails each day – and that is set to increase.[3] If you use a smartphone for work, then on average you're interacting with work for 13.5 hours every workday (72 hours per week, including weekend work).[4]

According to one report, this 'always on' culture means we have only about three hours on workdays for so-called 'discretionary' activities, such as being with our family, exercising and even showering (although the latter might hardly be considered discretionary!).[5]

Some of us have come to associate time with money in a way that encourages us to feel more and more pressured. We can feel an eternal need to make every moment economically worthwhile.[6] We can find ourselves unhealthily preoccupied with the cost of not working.

But apart from money, what drives the need to be so busy? The diagram below sets out some common assumptions that AIM helps us to examine a little more closely.

- Others will think of me as a better person if I am as busy (and I will too)
- If I work harder and harder, I will get more done
- If I multitask I will get more done
- If I stay busy I will keep things under control

⏱ HOW BUSY ARE YOU?

- When people ask you how you are, how frequently do you describe yourself as 'busy'?
- Would you like others to describe you as 'busy'? Why? What are your assumptions here?
- To what extent do you feel in a permanent state of 'catch-up' – never really being on top of things?
- When was the last time you took time to really reflect on your working life and why you do what you do?
- Do you feel there are 'rules' regarding when you should be 'at your desk' and that you are assessed according to whether you comply?
- To what extent would you describe yourself as a multitasker?

- Looking at your diary, how much 'space' is there?
- When did you last come into work despite being ill?
- To what extent do you feel the pressure to work outside 'normal' working hours?

By becoming curious about our experience we become more aware about how we think, feel, sense and habitually react.

'I'm a better person if I'm busy'

Saying we're busy can be a marker of our importance – 'I am so important, successful and *needed* that I am just rushed off my feet …!' Somehow, some of us have managed to develop a belief that being busy is the only way to be successful; if we have time to take a holiday (and only 6 out of 10 American workers use all their vacation time), or read a good book, then we clearly must be doing something wrong![7,8] Politicians, such as Donald Trump, and famous business people such as Marissa Mayer, previously the CEO of Yahoo!, the American technology company, have emphasised their capacity for getting up at 4 a.m., operating on just four hours' sleep, implying this is a sign of success. Signalling with pride our multitasking capabilities as a parent – being able to taxi three kids in different directions at the same time whilst organising the shopping and project managing the household renovations – is seen as the ultimate sign of success.

Worryingly, though, even if some of us, like Linda, suspect we are not being productive, there is a need to be seen to be busy because we are fearful of losing our job. This leads to the issue of presenteeism – being at work despite being ill because we're worried we might be fired if we aren't there. This costs employers enormous amounts – a Work Foundation report in the UK suggested that the loss in workplace productivity is greater as a result of presenteeism than as a result of absenteeism.[9]

'If I work harder, I get more done'

Ironically, far from there being a positive correlation between busyness and success, there comes a point when there is more likely to be a vicious circle of busyness, a decline in health and lower productivity. A study in the British *Lancet* medical journal suggests that if we work over 55 hours a week, our risk of stroke is 33 per cent higher, and of coronary heart disease 13 per cent higher, compared to those working 35 to 40 hours a week.[10] And there are any number of studies linking overwork to diabetes, depression, sleep disorders and early death.[11]

As we work harder and longer, instead of producing more and more we produce less and less, and we undermine our ability to think creatively and respond to changing circumstances.

How many hours a week do you work on average?

If it is around 50 hours your productivity may well be declining. If it is over 55 hours your productivity may be plummeting. If you are working about 70 hours a week, you may be producing the same output as your colleague who is on 56 hours a week.[12]

So what do we do with this conundrum as we notice we just aren't getting enough done? As Chapter 7 details, we very often just put our head down and, deluded, we work harder still!

Or we try to multitask.

'If I multitask I'll get more done'

Another reason to be busy comes from our persistent misplaced belief that multitasking helps us to do more. We spend only half our waking hours focused on the task we are actually undertaking.[13] During the rest of the time our mind wanders off. Nearly two-thirds of us do other activities while on conference calls, hopefully keeping just enough of our attention on the call to pick up when our name is mentioned.[14] We sit in meetings thinking about the next meeting, and three-quarters of us admit to doing other work in meetings (although these points may also say something about the nature of so many workplace meetings, of course).[15] The average worker spends only three minutes at a time on one task before they switch to something else.[16] Almost half of mums state they constantly juggle multiple tasks throughout the day.[17] And if you are juggling emails and work tasks it can lower your IQ by 10 points – more than smoking marijuana.[18]

All this in the belief that we can pack more in working this way.

As we multitask to get more done, we get less done. Our response? To work harder. To try harder at multitasking … and so the hamster wheel continues to spin, and we spend more time doing less.

We keep trying to get to a place where we feel in control.

'If I stay busy I will keep things under control'

Much of our busyness comes from our attempts to stay in control in what sometimes seems like a more and more unmanageable world. Recent remarkable economic and political changes show us how unpredictable and turbulent things can be and, as we are increasingly connected and interdependent, we feel shocks to the system in ways we never did previously.

We do not know what's around the corner and how it might affect demand for our work, whatever we do. This is not a comfortable position. We try to respond urgently and work harder to feel we are more secure.

As human beings we like to feel in control, and we will work hard to try and maintain this feeling. We chase outcomes faster and faster, and look over our shoulder and see others doing the same. So the sense of urgency cranks up a notch, as it did in Linda's organisation. 'If I don't work harder and harder, then I will get left behind and let people down.' It becomes a race to see who has the stamina to keep up the pace the longest.

We give ourselves little space to pause and reflect, as is shown in this story told by Stephen Covey:[19]

Suppose you were to come upon someone in the woods working feverishly to saw down a tree.

'What are you doing?' you ask.

'Can't you see?' comes the impatient reply. 'I'm sawing down this tree.'

'You look exhausted!' you exclaim. 'How long have you been at it?'

'Over five hours,' he replies, 'and I'm beat! This is hard work.'

'Well, why don't you take a break for five minutes and sharpen that saw?' you ask. 'I'm sure you would go a lot faster.'

'I don't have enough time to sharpen the saw,' the man says emphatically. 'I'm far too busy sawing!'

At work, we can find ourselves being too busy to realise we are being too busy. Busy trying to do things right rather than the right things. And it costs us as well as those we work with and for.

We need to step out of automatic busyness. Something needs to change.

Have you found your favourite Mind Time practice yet?

It's great to go with what seems easiest and most attractive. And it's also good to try other things out to broaden your range of skills.

AIM TO CHANGE YOUR MIND ABOUT BUSYNESS

To tackle these issues more productively, we can use AIM to help us to step out of automatic busyness in order to make more considered choices.

AIM develops our ability to notice the assumptions we make about our busyness and to question them. Developing our inquiry and meta-awareness helps us to spot our thoughts as simply thoughts rather than indisputable 'truth'. For example, we have more chance of questioning our thoughts as they arise, pausing and saying, 'Hang on – is it really true that I am getting more done by switching tasks?' 'Is it really true that being this busy means I am leading a meaningful, successful life?' Allowing then ensures we don't disappear down self-defeating self-critical pathways – 'Don't be so weak – of course you must stay busy!' or 'You just can't stand the heat, can you? Why can't you be as good as …?'

Sometimes we experience busyness as fulfilling and rewarding. Sometimes we would like to be busier or at least more challenged than we are currently. (Robert, whose story we told at the beginning of this chapter, felt this way.) As we become more aware, using AIM, we start to learn how and why we feel this way and to make appropriate choices.

But AIM also helps us to pick up, early on, the signs that our busyness is damaging our mental or physical health. We begin to spot unhealthy thoughts and physical pains rather than glossing over them in automatic pilot. We can then AIM to choose to use 'downtime' more effectively in order to rejuvenate. We talk about this much more in Chapter 7, which examines work–life balance.

Finally, with the practices of AIM, we can choose to focus on one task at a time in order to be more productive, rather than automatically seeking, and usually failing, to multitask. We notice when our attention moves away from the task in hand and so we have the opportunity to refocus.

Let's move now to the second area where we can find ourselves caught in automatic reactions – change.

ALL CHANGE!

Heraclitus, an ancient Greek philosopher, wrote in the sixth century BC that 'change is the only constant in life', and while adaptation has always been a critical ingredient of personal and organisational success, there is a general perception that the pace of change is accelerating. We are putting a premium on speed.[20]

It might be that in your work you are asked to do things differently, or to do different things more frequently and faster. Some of these changes may be small – a new way of billing customers, a new way of logging time, a new way of accessing or sharing information on the intranet. Some, however, may be more significant – changing your job role in the new restructuring or promotion, or learning an entirely new way to use technology to do things. Like Linda, you may be dealing with more than one change as the world of work sometimes seems to be in a permanently volatile state – before one change reaches its conclusion another one ignites.

In Chapter 8 we will explore in more detail the impact of change and unexpected events. Here, we introduce a helpful model called The Four Rooms of Change. Developed by Claes Janssen, a Swedish psychologist, it shows our common, automatic reaction to change in the workplace. Used alongside AIM it helps us to spot and make sense of our experience and to make perhaps more compassionate choices in the way we treat ourselves and others in our work.[21]

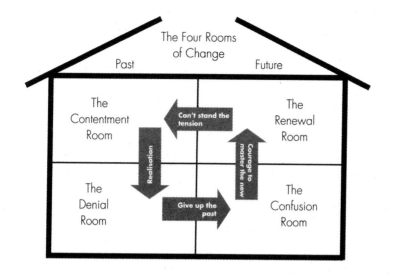

We can start in any room but let's say we are in Contentment. We feel relatively comfortable with our work and, having been working flat out, it is only natural that we seize the chance to take our foot off the accelerator. We begin to feel pleased with ourselves and in control. But then something happens – a realisation – more change has come; a trap door opens and we fall into the Denial room. We resist, fight back – it can't be like this, things were going so well! Perhaps if we put our heads down it will go away …

Eventually we acknowledge that the old ways of doing things are gone for ever and change is inevitable. We enter the Confusion room. We don't yet understand what or how we need to do things. After a time, though, we climb into the Renewal room where we master new ways of doing things, regain purpose and again feel more positive and excited. But as we find we can't maintain this energy and pace for ever, we slip back into contentment, allowing ourselves to relax. And so the cycle continues.

As we have already mentioned, we are unlikely to experience just one change at a time, and so we might find ourselves in different rooms at different points relating to different changes.

However, this emotional experience of change continues without end – contentment, denial, confusion and renewal.

We can allow ourselves to be swept up in these emotions, our well-being slavishly dependent upon external circumstances, or, through practising AIM, we can allow ourselves more choice in how we respond.

AIM TO CHANGE YOUR MIND ABOUT CHANGE

The world is changing more rapidly than ever before. It is inevitable that we will continue to be affected in our work by changing technology, expectations and ways of doing things. While we can't necessarily influence those changes too much, what we do have influence over is our response to them. Let's see how we can AIM to help ourselves.

First, helping ourselves through change processes productively is impossible to do well if we find ourselves caught up in making stress-inducing judgements of ourselves or others around us. Particularly in the Denial and Confusion rooms, it is common to feel frustrated with ourselves, others or the situation – or all of the above! It is *very* common to wish things were other than they are. An attitude of allowing, compassion and just a little humour, helped along by keeping things in perspective, can help us through difficult times. This sort of attitude is the one we practise, time and again, in Mind Time so that, when we need it most, we can access it naturally and easily.

Second, inquiring into our experience of change helps us to see which change room we are in. That in turn gives us a bit more perspective and understanding about our situation. Rather than being caught in loops of contentment, denial or anxiety, our meta-awareness helps us to observe our thoughts, feelings, sensations and impulses. As soon as we do that we have stepped out of automatic reactivity and into a place where we can choose, if needed, a more thoughtful response.

Our reactions when things are changing at work are often linked to previous experiences, which may mean we automatically tend to feel positive about change or resigned or afraid. An exercise alongside AIM that we sometimes use with people seeking to inquire into their assumptions is shown here.

WHAT ARE MY ASSUMPTIONS ABOUT CHANGE?

Pause and consider the images shown below.

If you had to pick one which resonates most with your reaction to change in the workplace, which one would you pick?

Then ask yourself these further questions:

- Why did you pick the picture and what does it tell you about your assumptions, expectations and experiences with change?

- How does the above affect how you approach change now?
- In general, what thoughts and emotions do you connect with change? Excitement? Weariness? Fear? Opportunity? If 'it depends', what does it depend on?
- What enables you to approach change productively?

Meta-awareness of our thoughts, feelings, sensations and impulses gives us clues as to where we are in the Four Rooms of Change. It gives us an indication of what it might take to move through the rooms and into Renewal. It also enables us to choose to look after ourselves better if we notice change is taking its toll.

Allowing, Inquiry and Meta-awareness, developed during Mind Time, are fundamental to shifting to an 'approach' response rather than an 'inhibited' reaction. They enable us to catch ourselves as our thoughts move towards wishing things were different or to unproductive blaming of others, who will not alter just because we want them to. They give us just that small space where we can get things back into perspective and become more curious about our experience.

Let's finally look at the last of the automatic reactions in the workplace that can expend quite a bit of our energy – keeping up appearances.

KEEPING UP APPEARANCES

In every workplace there are what we call 'the rules of the game'. The way things are done and should be done. These rules are usually not explicitly written down – we just pick them up. They can be helpful and energising, or they can be pressurising and cause stress.

In Linda's case that we described at the start of this chapter, she felt she could not possibly show that she felt exhausted because that was just not what she 'should' do. To be successful, in her mind, she 'should' be confident and definitely busy. Rightly or wrongly, that was the implicit message she was picking up at work.

The problem was she felt neither of those things, and so she decided to present a façade – acting out an Oscar-winning performance, fitting to expectations. In the words of the philosopher Martin Buber, she was spending her time 'seeming' rather than 'being' in an attempt to be accepted.[22]

In Robert's case, he was also keeping up appearances. He was keeping up the appearance of being engaged enough to make sure he was still seen as promotable and respected.

Pretending to be engaged and pretending to be confident are two of the most common façades we present in the workplace. They take energy to maintain and can cause us anxiety and unease. Much of the time we don't even know we are presenting them, so ingrained are our automatic assumptions about how we need to appear to others.

Pretending to be engaged

Day-in and day-out many of us do the same sorts of things, yet those whom we work with do not necessarily want to see that we ever get bored. We are often expected to put an enthusiastic smile on our face. But research by Gallup shows that 70 per cent of us are actually disengaged at work.[23]

One reason for feeling disengaged is the relationship we have with the powerful people in our workplace. Our manager, our key work colleague or our most important customer or supplier influences our motivation enormously and, let's face it, many of us are just stuck with the ones we have. But, given they are often responsible for our pay, promotion, workload or opportunities, we can feel forced into appearing to be engaged and enthusiastic even if we sometimes can find them frustrating, distant, micromanaging or uncaring.

Another reason for disengagement is boredom – a state of mind that, over time, can be damaging to our health. Some of us are bored because we crave constant stimulation and change. Some of us, a bit like Robert, are bored because we have retreated from riskier endeavours because we are fearful of them and are left, as a result, with a boring job. Some of us are simply in positions where we do not feel we can tap into the opportunities for more stimulating work.

Whatever the reason, boredom costs us – it is associated with alcohol abuse, smoking, comfort eating and even premature death.[24] If, however, we feel trapped, unable to change our work situation but scared of losing our job, we might use a lot of energy putting on a show to others that we are busy and enthusiastic even if we feel bored stiff.

It can feel intensely risky to drop the façade, to admit to being disengaged. Perhaps catastrophising the results, Robert felt that if he let on even a little bit that he was bored he might lose his job – or he might be given a role that would take away his valued flexibility.

Pretending that we are confident

Have you ever thought that you don't deserve your success? That you're not as good at your job as others think you are and any minute now you'll be found out as a fraud? That your success is the result mainly of luck, others' work or timing?

Hearing this sort of 'inner voice' of doubt is very common. It has been coined the 'impostor phenomenon'.[25] It often coincides with placing huge expectations on ourselves to be perfect. Striving hard to prove to ourselves and to others that we *are* capable rather than impostors, we end up getting good results, which serve to just pile on further pressure to live up to expectations.

An element of impostor phenomenon is entirely normal and ensures we still possess humility – there is nothing wrong with a bit of self-deprecation. If we never doubt ourselves and live with a grandiose sense of self we may technically be termed a psychopath (and indeed, this term possibly correctly applies to between 3 and 20 per cent of business leaders, depending on which study you look at).[26,27,28] But, when the impostor phenomenon tips over to chronic self-doubt which we attempt to hide using a confident façade, it can be very damaging and anxiety provoking.

Even Sheryl Sandberg, as chief operating officer of Facebook, number one on the *Forbes* list of most powerful women in technology and with a self-made worth of over \$1 billion, is not immune to this. She publicly admitted to feeling like an impostor despite the enormous evidence suggesting the opposite, saying, 'There are still days when I wake up feeling like a fraud, not sure I should be where I am.'[29]

Similarly, Linda felt like she would be found out as incapable at any moment. She thought she needed to look confident, but she just didn't feel it. So her energy was being diverted into keeping up appearances.

Whether we are keeping up the appearance of engagement or confidence – or indeed any other façade – the practices of allowing, inquiry and meta-awareness can help us to reassess, reduce anxiety and choose a more productive response.

AIM TO CHANGE YOUR MIND ABOUT KEEPING UP APPEARANCES

We can AIM to deal more productively with the need to be seen a certain way:

- Allowing helps us to be kind to ourselves and others. Beating ourselves up about a lack of confidence, for example, does not improve the situation!
- Inquiring helps us to explore and learn about how 'rules of the game', 'façade' and 'impostor experiences' might affect us. Rather than ignore these things, we learn to be interested and curious.
- Meta-awareness helps us to observe, in the moment, how we think, feel and act in ways that are led by the need to perform – and to notice where we have the choice to do something other than succumb to automatic pilot.

In these ways AIM helps us to tune into the little voice in our heads that might put pressure on us to keep up appearances.

🕐 THE LITTLE VOICE INSIDE OUR HEAD

How you would complete these sentences? Notice how you think and feel as you answer:

At work, in order to be recognized as successful, I should be …

The things I could not possibly admit to feeling and thinking are …

I want people to see me as …

I absolutely do not want people to see me as …

> What people at work don't know about me is that I feel ...
> What people at work don't know about me is that I think ...
> Typically, if I face an opportunity that stretches me I think to myself ...

The little voice inside our head is so influential in how we behave and how we perform at work and in our lives generally. It can be a friend – a companion who coaches us to allow – to be gentle with ourselves – and tells us that we can do it. Or it can be that 'poison parrot' that sees threats more than opportunities, that undermines our confidence by pointing out our failings and criticises any attempts to do things differently.

When we tune into the voice and see it for what it is – just a voice that is not the 'truth' – then we open up choice. We can choose whether to listen, whether to react, whether to respond differently, whether to be more kind to ourselves.

If that voice reminds us frequently that we are bored at work, we might either accept that as true and inevitable, or we might see it as a stimulus to inquire into what we can do that might make things more interesting. So boredom might be something we succumb to, which depresses us and brings us down, or it could become a driver to push us to seek opportunities.

When, with AIM, we hear the 'impostor' voice narrating the last time we messed up and therefore why we should not step forward this time, perhaps we can choose to recall an example of when we succeeded instead. We know that people rarely regret taking on new, more challenging roles that initially seem daunting – they just regret not taking them. We also know that we have real strengths. We can remind ourselves of these things.

Practising AIM means we are able to notice our inner voice as it speaks. We are able to encourage our allowing, compassionate voice to be heard a bit more often. We can amplify the inquiring 'approach' voice more than the pressuring and anxious 'inhibited' voice.

We are then in a place where we can more easily choose our response.

Do you find yourself getting frustrated by the way your mind wanders in Mind Time?

Remember – it really is just what minds tend to do. It's how we are. Each time you notice the mind has wandered is a small moment of meta-awareness. If you have lots of those moments, you're building your capacity for that, and that's excellent!

There is a great deal that can be done to improve our effectiveness at work. This chapter has explored three very common ways we deplete our energy unnecessarily by being in automatic pilot – our busyness, our response to change, and the lengths we go to in order to keep up appearances. We may never altogether eliminate these, but we can AIM to choose different courses of action that will enable us to thrive rather than just survive at work.

KEY MESSAGES IN CHAPTER 5

- There are three common automatic reactions at work which deplete our resilience and distract us but where AIM can help: being too busy, getting unhealthily caught up in fighting changes which we may not be able to influence, and seeking to keep up appearances to please others.
- AIM helps us to identify and then question our assumptions about being busy. It helps us to spot when busyness is healthy and when it is leading to mental and physical illness. And it helps us to prioritise and focus on tasks more effectively.
- AIM helps us to notice and accept that our experience of change at work can be emotional – we are perpetually experiencing a cycle of contentment, denial, confusion and renewal. AIM enables us to spot our automatic reactions and, if needed, choose more appropriate responses to change.
- Many of us construct a façade to live up to expectations in the workplace which often drive us to appear confident, enthusiastic and capable at all times. Underneath this façade, however, many of us experience boredom and/or the feeling of being an impostor. AIM helps us to tune into the little voice in our head which drives these sorts of feelings. We can develop a more kindly voice towards ourselves and others – and this in turn encourages us to learn and try things at a deeper level.

Chapter 6

AIM for
Better Health

GET ACTIVE

Hippocrates, the Father of Modern Medicine, is said to have been the first person to recognise that diseases came from natural causes, not from the gods, and he understood the body's natural powers of recuperation. If we all had 'the right amount of nourishment and exercise, not too little and not too much, we would have found the safest way to health,' he said.

It seems so obvious. But in the 2,000 years since Hippocrates' advice, we haven't been all that good at following it. Instead we've taken another path.

When it comes to exercise, physical inactivity has grown to become the fourth largest global killer in the world.[1] That's partly due to its links with the development of heart disease, type 2 diabetes, obesity, depression, dementia and cancer.[2]

We all know we ought to be more active, and for many of us being inactive can make us feel bad about ourselves. We feel guilty and frustrated, and often try to appease those feelings by giving in to the 'reward' of yet more inactivity. We blob out on the couch with snacks and a box set, looking for comfort, rest and freedom from stress. And that doesn't work. It doesn't make us healthier or happier.

How can we fix this? Clearly, scolding ourselves and sternly telling ourselves that we ought to be more active doesn't help. We've all done plenty of that. Here's something that might actually help: when we enjoy something, we're much more likely to do it.

Science (as well as our own experience) tells us that when we're more mindful we're more likely to enjoy activity. Researchers in Holland analysed the experience of physical activity of around 400 people.[3] They found that the more mindful people were while they were physically active, the more satisfied they were by that activity. That, they reckon, is simply because they enjoyed it more!

When you're more mindful, you're more aware of the positive emotions you experience.[4,5] The more aware you are of those positive emotions, the more satisfied you feel. The more satisfaction you get from any new activity the more likely you are to continue with it.[6] And that might explain why researchers in another study found that mindfulness helps people to stay physically active.[7]

So, if you're currently inactive and you want to improve your chances of living a long, healthy and happy life, get active and use the skills you're building up through your daily Mind Time to help you enjoy that activity. If you're currently very inactive, you'll need to build up to that gradually. But whatever you do, you're much more likely to keep it up if you choose activities you enjoy.

Research suggests we would all benefit from around 150 minutes of moderate activity every week, and strength exercises that work all our major muscles on two or more days a week.[8] Moderate activity is any activity that raises your heart rate and makes you breathe faster and feel warmer. You're working at a moderate level if you can still talk, but you can't sing the words to a song.

How does this sound to you?

Do you think 'What? How am I going to fit that in, when you're already telling me to meditate every day?'

Or maybe 'Come on, that's nothing. I'd never have run a marathon last year if I only did that!'

Or are you somewhere in between?

Wherever you find yourself on that spectrum, bring AIM to bear. Allow yourself to feel however you're feeling. Inquire into what's going on here – what habits of mind are in play right now? And use meta-awareness to notice more deeply your own reactions, whatever they are.

And if you want to get more active, you can use AIM to help you enjoy that activity.

> **Do you sometimes feel sleepy during Mind Time?**
>
> **If so, you're certainly not alone in that.**
>
> **Maybe try a different posture – or a different time of day.**

I (Michael) live in Cambridge and often commute to London. I use the train to make the 50-minute journey to London and back. The journey by bus or taxi from my home to Cambridge Station through the congested streets is barely faster than the 25-minute walk. So, unless I have heavy bags to manage, I walk. Not only does that save me money and reduce carbon emissions, it also increases my levels of activity. But more than that – on the days that I walk, so long as it's not pouring with rain, I usually arrive at the station feeling much better than I would have had I driven. Walking helps me to connect more deeply with myself and with the world around me.

How could you custom-build a version of this for yourself?

First, and perhaps most importantly, there is the issue of attitude and intention. I set out on my 25-minute brisk walk with the clear intention of using the opportunity to increase my level of daily activity as well as my present-moment awareness.

That means deliberately not listening to music or anything else on headphones and keeping my smartphone firmly in my pocket for the duration of the walk. If I leave the house having just sent an important email to a client, and I feel the itch to know they've received it, I try to make a point of just noticing that itch, experiencing it, and then choose not to go with it. Whatever that little smartphone-itch whispers in my inner ear, there's nothing going on that can't wait for 25 minutes!

Then, I also set out with the intention of enjoying the walk. It is an opportunity to put the daily hassles aside, or at least get them into a wider perspective. It's an opportunity to engage with the ebb and flow of life apart from my daily preoccupations. Using the inquiry element of AIM, I might notice the changing quality of light, the changing of the seasons. I enjoy exchanging greetings with my neighbours and seeing the neighbourhood cats working out their territories.

But this is a brisk walk, so very soon I start to notice changes in my body. Here, the meta-awareness part of AIM comes to the fore. My heart rate inches up and I might notice that. I may start needing to manage my breathing ever so slightly, and sometimes I notice and enjoy that. The fact that I'm now breathing slightly more consciously helps me to check in with my current emotional state. I scan my body, looking for any tensing or holding. If I notice any, I can make a choice. I might breathe with it, breathe into it, see if it will ease and move; or I might inquire into it – 'What's this tension all about? What's bothering me right now?' That can help me to become clearer about what's going on with me; it can help me to be more present and in better shape for whatever comes next.

I might also use the walk as a way of mentally preparing for whatever I'm going to do in London. Importantly, this doesn't mean that I plan what I'm going to say or think yet again about my schedule. Rather, it involves getting into the right frame of mind for what's coming up. This calls more upon the allowing dimension of AIM – especially the compassion aspect of allowing. So sometimes I might call to mind the people I'll be meeting, cultivating feelings of warm goodwill towards them, much as in the loving-kindness practice we discussed in Chapter 3 (see page 63–6). And I nudge myself into an optimistic frame of mind around what's coming up. I might briefly imagine myself at the end of an upcoming event that has gone well, and enjoy the feelings that come with that.

But that work preparation is only ever a small part of the 25-minute walk. When it's out of the way, I consciously return my attention to the ever-changing present-moment experience. And I do that over and over again throughout the walk.

The way I use my attention on the walk has some similarities to the way we suggest you use your attention in the Present Moment awareness practice we have shared in the downloads. Rather than directing my attention at any single focus, my main intention is simply to stay present with whatever emerges into the field of experience, and to return to that no matter how many times my mind takes me away from the present.

The feeling of my feet striking the pavement, the sense of warmth or coolness in the air, the colours of the doors of the houses I'm passing, the feeling of mutual delight passing between a mother and her toddler, the chatter of school-kids cycling by. Attending to all and any of these present-moment experiences in tiny and incremental ways increases my enjoyment on the walk.

It's important that these small moments of enjoyment are allowed to be small. We don't need to make a big deal of them. They are the micro-moments of positivity that our Teflon-like positivity receptors easily allow to slide away, barely noticed. But when we cultivate, even to a small extent, the habit of noticing and savouring them, they begin to add up and we find that even something as relatively mundane as a walk to the railway station can end up being really enjoyable.

Of course, when we're engaged in a simple activity like walking we don't only find our attention dwelling on experiences of the outside world. Thoughts, feelings, memories – various forms of mental activity puff up out of nowhere. When that happens, we can treat the passing thoughts or memories much as we do any other experience on the walk. They're just experiences to notice and pass by. The meta-awareness part of AIM is very useful here.

If you've been doing your Mind Time (and we hope you have), you'll know the difference now between 'noticing' a thought and 'thinking' a thought. The act of noticing, of witnessing thoughts and feelings without needing to engage with them, is one of the key skills that can enable us to stay present during any simple activity. If we start to get lost in thought, we are no longer present. We are just walking and thinking. And although that may be useful and even sometimes productive, it isn't enjoyable in the same way and we do not get the added benefits of strengthening our overall capacity to AIM.

If we can build an activity like this regularly into our day or our week we get three benefits:

1. We become more active and get the health benefits of that.
2. We turn something like a routine walk into a Mind Time practice, and we get the added benefits of that.
3. We enjoy life more.

What's not to like about that? It builds our physical and mental health.

So far, we've been focusing on the shift from being inactive to becoming moderately active – and to bringing AIM to that process. But some of us want more than that. You may already be moderately active and you might even be very active. How might you use your capacities for AIM to take these states still further?

Megan's husband Steve swims to keep fit. Sometimes it feels enjoyable; sometimes it feels like hard work. A while ago Steve began to wonder whether he was pushing himself too much as a minor injury in his arm began to bother him. He decided to pay more attention while he was swimming. He decided to AIM to improve both his swimming technique and to increase his enjoyment, sensing that these were connected.

So, using AIM, he began to notice his attitude towards his swimming – noticing when he berated himself for what he considered poor swimming and instead tuning in to inquiring into what his present-moment experience was like. So for a few lengths he would focus on the sensations of the water running past his hands as he took a stroke. Then he shifted attention on to the slow rocking motion of his body during the front crawl. He became far more attuned to his technique – not in a 'telling off' way, but rather in an interested and curious way.

He noticed that, when he swam with this quality of attention, his swimming felt natural and at ease. He enjoyed it far more. And, interestingly, he also swam faster.

SLEEP

When we teach the practices we've discussed in this book there is one theme that we hear over and over again. 'Soon after I close my eyes I start to fall asleep.'

There may be many different reasons for this, but one thing is clear – in general, most of us today aren't getting enough sleep.

Shift work, the need to work across different time zones simultaneously, and international travel are all common causes of sleep loss.[9] On top of this, the use of artificial lighting and hand-held technologies at night, an ever-increasing pressure to perform at work (and to be 'seen' to perform), as well as the lengthening of the working day all make the challenge of getting optimal sleep much more difficult.[10]

Research by the American Academy of Sleep Science tells us that the minimum number of hours of sleep required for a healthy adult is 7 (they recommend a range of between 7 and 9 hours).[11]

Our colleague at Ashridge, Vicki Culpin, has spent the last 10 years researching the issue of sleep and work.[12] What she has found is important for all of us. According to Vicki, the executives she surveyed were getting an average of only 6 hours 28 minutes. This lack of sleep affects people's health, their social lives and their lives at work – especially when it comes to tasks that need sustained attention. Decision-making, creativity, information processing, adaptability, learning and control of emotions are all diminished by sleep loss.

When they weren't getting enough sleep, the people Vicki surveyed reported that they

- were less able to stay focused
- took longer to complete tasks
- found it harder to work with particularly challenging colleagues
- found it challenging to generate new ideas
- were less able to manage competing demands
- found it harder to have difficult conversations
- were less effective at forming opinions, and
- completed tasks to a lower standard than they normally would.

Above all, people speak of finding the interpersonal aspects of work particularly challenging when they've not had enough sleep. People who experience this withdraw socially, and that affects them, their customers, teams and organisations.

When we don't get enough sleep, we feel lethargic. That brings slower reaction times and poorer vision. That's especially dangerous for people such as drivers, surgeons or others whose work requires fast reactions. But whatever work we do, a lack of sleep reduces the amount of energy we have available. Not only that. Sleeplessness increases levels of stress, and for most people it also produces anxiety.

Vicki and her team studied the impact of sleeplessness at work – but that must also be mirrored by people's experience at home. A lack of sleep disrupts home life just as much as it does life at work.

What to do about this?

First, it's important to pay attention to basic sleep habits. The UK's National Health Service offers these 10 tips for improving these:[13]

1. Try to establish regular sleep hours.
2. Pay attention to your sleeping environment.
3. Make sure your bed is comfortable.
4. Get regular exercise.
5. Cut down on caffeine.
6. Don't over-indulge in food or alcohol.
7. Don't smoke.
8. Take a little time to unwind before going to bed.
9. Come away from all LED screens at least 60 minutes before bedtime.
10. If you can't sleep, get up.

And they advise that if lack of sleep is persistent and affecting your daily life, make an appointment to see your doctor.

All of this is good advice. Added to it, there are the benefits of the Mind Time practices we've shared. People we've worked with tell us that one of the biggest impacts of doing these regularly is that their sleep improves. Research studies bear this out.[14]

So, if you're falling asleep during Mind Time, we recommend all the above. But there is something else on offer too.

In the Mind Time classes we teach, people tell us that when they fall asleep while practising it's not as if they're fully awake one moment and fully asleep the next moment. Instead, most people speak of passing through a kind of 'in-between state' – not quite fully awake, not quite asleep.

Sleep scientists and psychologists call this the 'hypnogogic state'. It comes from the Greek word *hupnos* – 'sleep' – added to *agogos* – 'leading'. The lovely thing about this word is that it conjures up that feeling of nodding that people sometimes have as they're about to fall asleep during Mind Time and they catch themselves and jerk away again. 'Gog' – your head nods down. 'Gog' – it jerks up again.

Words aside, there are two wonderful and really valuable things about the in-between state.[15]

First, it can be a great introduction to the wonders and complexities of the mind and its depths. As we enter this in-between state, images will often start to bubble up into the conscious mind with a strange, dream-like quality. Attending to these with some degree of awareness can give us an insight into the complex depths of your mind. Artists like Salvador Dalí and creative thinkers like the inventor Thomas Edison consciously used the in-between state as a way of generating ideas and images.[16] Second, if we AIM to take the time to become more familiar with our own experience of the in-between state – allowing it to be as it is; inquiring, curious and interested in the changing images and experiences that emerge; and meta-aware of the changing play of our minds – then we can begin to use that familiarity to help us to fall asleep when we need to. With time and practice we can summon up and enter that in-between state a bit more at will. And, because it is the doorway into sleep, it can help us to fall asleep much more easily.

When sleep doesn't come easily it's easy to fall into a self-defeating spiral of anxiety. 'Oh no! It's 4 a.m. and I've still not slept! I'm going to be so tired tomorrow – and I've got so much on my to-do list!'

With AIM, we can more easily notice those anxious thoughts and feelings as *just* anxious thoughts and feelings. Seeing how they really don't help in cases like this, maybe we can put them gently aside for a time.

Or maybe we can do something more helpful still. Allowing the situation to be as it is, using our meta-awareness to see what's going on in our thoughts and feelings that are keeping us awake, we can try to move our attention more deliberately into the body. Coming away from the anxious thoughts and feelings that often kick off in the small hours, we can begin to explore our body sensations with a kindly curiosity. We can't be curious and anxious at the same time, and when we're exploring sensations in the body, we're not thinking – or not very much. Keeping our attention in the body, we might feel our toes, our calves, our buttocks and back in contact with the bed. Sensing our arms and fingers, the back of our head – whatever's there. Keeping our attention with the body can calm the anxious mind. Sometimes it can be a way of slipping back into sleep.

DIET

'Not too little, not too much,' said Hippocrates. How ironic, then, that after years when food shortage was a widespread global killer (and many still don't get enough to eat), by 2012 the number of years of healthy living lost as a result of people eating too much outweighed the number lost by people eating too little.[17] And while most of us seem to be concerned with the changes to our appearance and body-shape that come along with weight gain, the long-term dangers of overeating are much more devastating than that. Overeating increases your risk of heart disease and type 2 diabetes, as well as the risks of developing certain types of cancer, gallbladder disease, sleep apnoea and stroke. No amount of knowing that we *should* change our diet actually helps us to change it, though. Cinzia Pezzolesi – a good friend – is a clinical psychologist. Part of her work consists in helping people to change the way they eat. Her book, *The Art of Mindful Eating*, challenges the solutions we have applied to dieting so far.[18] These, she thinks, have become problematic.

Eating, she says, is an art, not a science. 'Sure, there is a lot of science behind the art of eating well – just as there is behind most art. But mindful eating is the art of developing a healthy, joyful and relaxed relationship with food, without the struggle. Of course developing this orientation towards food will take time to build.

'Your body has a natural self-regulating mechanism,' she told us, and having recently had a baby she has seen this mechanism in action before it gets over-ridden by other parts of the human system. 'When Leonardo doesn't want to eat, he closes his mouth and gives me that look – "I don't want this …" – but somehow, as we grow up we lose that instinctual capacity. It's as if we start to eat with our minds, not our bodies.'

Restrictive diets like paleo or 5:2 are ways of trying to control our bodies with our minds. Diets like this are created with good intent and they sometimes work well. But they can also be confusing. After all, they're subject to trends and fashions. Every year there's a new diet and a new approach becomes dominant. But our body-wisdom doesn't change. If we can tune into that, it offers us a stable source of knowing what, and what not, to eat.

Cinzia shared with us a combined Mindful Eating practice that covers three aspects of mindful eating:

- Eating with all your senses
- Connecting with the self-regulating mechanism of hunger
- Enjoyment

You can use this as a 'bite-size' practice before approaching a meal, or as a 'mindful bite' practice to use with a snack.

⏱ MINDFUL EATING

Find a comfortable posture, rest your hands on your lap, and close your eyes if you wish. Take a few intentional breaths, notice the flow of air that enters the nostrils, travels down into the lungs and gently flows back out again.

How does your body feel right now?

Now gently focus your attention around the area of your stomach. How hungry are you?

On a scale of 1 to 10, where 1 is not hungry at all and 10 is as hungry as possible, what is your number?

Notice the cues that your body gives you to tell you that it is hungry.

Take a moment to look at your food, bring awareness to its shape, colour and unique characteristics.

Explore the aroma of what you are about to eat, and when you are ready take your first mindful bite.

Sense the texture, the flavour, the temperature of the food …

Really pay attention to the sensations in your mouth.

Notice your reactions … any liking, disliking or judgement.

Let yourself observe these feelings and thoughts as you remain fully aware and mindful.

Continue to eat at your natural pace, checking in from time to time with your hunger.

Give yourself permission to enjoy this meal or snack without any guilt or self-criticism; after all, you are treating your body with respect by eating when you are hungry.

Research tells us that when you use practices such as Mind Time, you're better able to tell when you have eaten enough and to make your judgements about whether or not to continue eating based on your actual experience of fullness. That's especially so if you do a brief check-in with yourself and your body before you start to eat.[19]

So, we can use AIM to help us decide when to stop eating. By allowing ourselves to eat more or to eat less, depending on how we actually feel; inquiring into whether we feel full or whether we're no longer enjoying what we were eating; and by being aware of what we're thinking, feeling and sensing – and whatever impulses are here – we can decide when we've had enough. Enjoying our food, we can appreciate what it's given to our bodies to provide them with energy and enhance our well-being.

AGEING

We're all growing older every moment, but we don't always see that. Sometimes it only becomes apparent to us when we realise that we have lost some of the capabilities we previously took for granted. Maybe we're that bit less able to remember where we've put something, or that bit less flexible. Perhaps we discover when we climb several flights of stairs that we're not quite as fit as we used to be. There are a few more wrinkles, a few more greying hairs. We might go to a school reunion and, with a shock, realise how much everyone has aged. Then we pause, reflect, and notice that we must have too.

Ageing is inevitable. AIM can make the process easier.

We gain nothing from denying the fact that we are getting older. It happens and we can't stop it. Here, the allowing part of AIM comes to the fore. We can try to fight the ageing process, treating it like an enemy consuming our youth and vigour, or we can embrace, allow and work with it more skilfully. We can start by seeing the positive sides of getting older – which we often don't acknowledge and which society ignores to a large extent.

According to Michael Ramscar, a cognitive neuroscientist based at the University of Tübingen, some of the apparent cognitive decline that comes with healthy ageing may be nothing more than the effects of our having gained more experience. We're slower because we have to deal with the consequences of our learning.

In other words, part of why some of us get slower when we're older is because we're actually smarter. As Ramscar puts it, 'Older adults' changing performance reflects memory search demands, which get bigger as people's experience grows.' In other words, as we get older, we gather more experiences, learn more names for things, and we have a better understanding of how the social and economic systems around us work. This can make us slower and more considered in our approach. Youth has speed and flexibility, but with age comes wisdom and guile.

This is not to downplay the fact that some of the cognitive decline some people experience as they age may be down to various forms of structural deterioration in the brain. But it's important also to see that what we might experience as a relative change of speed in ourselves or in those we know might not be due to such changes. It could just be that we all have more to process as we age.

In any event, we need to allow that with age we most likely slow down.

The inquiry part of AIM also has a powerful part to play in enabling us to grow old with more ease and grace. Here the point is that this moment now, *this* moment, that is our life. However old we are, it's easy to fall into a habit of looking back and thinking our best days are behind us, that life belongs to those younger than us. Not so. This moment, this is all any of us have. Right here, right now. This is it. This is our life – not our life in the past. When we've trained our capacity to AIM, even a bit more, we can more easily keep our attention in the present moment more often. We can get interested in, and curious about, what's here now. To the extent that we can really live in the present and embrace the life we have right now, with all its richness – its ups and downs, joys and pains – then age may be less of an issue.

Of course, as we age we don't always only look back to a more gilded time. I (Michael) was once at an event where I was part of a small team training professional mindfulness teachers. The event took place in a stunning mountain landscape, alongside a beautiful lake. Most of the participants were mental health professionals who were looking to the training to guide them in using mindfulness to help patients or clients in healthcare services. They had the kind of professional demeanour one might expect. But one woman stood out from the crowd. In her mid-50s, her hair was wild, her clothing eccentric – and she had tattoos in places that would not be easily concealed by professional garb. In a break, I asked her what had brought her to the training. A heart-wrenching story unfolded.

She told me that she'd grown up in the care system, which was tough. Then she'd been adopted, but her adoptive parents died and she was returned to care. The story that followed was marked by a pattern of constant, heart-breaking loss and betrayal.

'I'm now in my mid-fifties, I've had no children, I've got no partner, no parents, no family. As I get older, there's no one who'll care for me. I've got no grandchildren to look forward to. It could be quite bleak. But, you know what? Right now, I'm OK. In this moment, I'm fine. In each present moment it's all OK. Through my mindfulness practice I've discovered that, and if I can keep my attention with that, then I'm OK. That discovery has been completely life-changing for me. It's allowed me to be happy and fulfilled. I want to share that with others. That's why I'm here.'

The inquiry part of AIM helps us to maintain that kind of present-centredness. We get more interested in, more engaged with, the present moment.

The meta-awareness aspect of AIM supports our capacity for allowing and inquiring by helping us to notice our thoughts, feelings, body sensations and impulses as they are right now just as thoughts, feelings, body sensations and impulses. We can notice any tendency to judge our ageing bodies with less than compassion and perhaps we can let go of that and find a warmer attitude. After all, our bodies have supported us over the years, perhaps through the birth of a child or during a stressful time at work or in highly competitive games. We can appreciate that and be kinder and more patient with ourselves.

When we notice ourselves (or older friends or relatives) fumbling for a thought or memory in ways we are unused to, AIM can help us to treat that with more kindness.

Allowing, Inquiry and Meta-awareness – they can help us to age more gracefully.

But there's more on offer from the practices in this book.

Recent scientific research tells us that just a few minutes of meditation every day improves the cognitive abilities in people aged 55 to 75 years old. This goes against the common belief that we all inevitably lose mental capacity over time. The researchers found that when people meditated for 10 to 15 minutes a day over 8 weeks, they became significantly quicker at returning their attention to a computer task they had been set when their attention was constantly disrupted.

It seems that even as we grow older we can continue to train our minds and change our brains. Which is wonderful news when you consider that many of you who are reading this book will live well into your hundreds!

> How is your Mind Time practice going?
>
> What helps that?
>
> What gets in the way?

MENTAL HEALTH – ANXIETY/DEPRESSION

Ruby Wax – a good friend of Michael's and a fellow mindfulness practitioner and author – built her name and reputation as a comedian on BBC television shows such as *The Full Wax* and *Ruby Wax Meets* … What wasn't widely known, though, was that for all her success and the laughs she attracted, most of her life Ruby struggled with often disabling depression.

For much of that time she thought of herself as somehow alone with her illness. 'It was a secret that you didn't want anyone to know about – there were feelings of shame attached to it.' In the grip of a particularly disabling episode, she checked into a clinic to get some help and finally realised how widespread mental health problems are. 'It's so common,' she told us, 'it could happen to anyone. But nobody wants to talk about it and that makes everything worse. Let's be open about it. I now say that one in five people have dandruff, one in four have mental health problems – I've had both.'

Ruby has written about depression and used the topic for her one-woman shows as a way of getting the subject out in the open. 'We need to take the stigma out of mental illness. People shouldn't be ashamed of it. It used to be the "C" word – cancer – that people wouldn't discuss. Now it's the "M" word. I hope pretty soon it'll be OK for everyone to talk openly about their mental health without fear of being treated differently.'

More recently, in the UK Prince Harry has spoken about the fact that he sought counselling after 20 years of bottling up his grief over his mother's death. In an interview[20] he spoke candidly about how he had suppressed his emotions after losing his mother, Princess Diana, when he was 12. Initially he took up boxing to help cope with feelings of aggression before finally seeking counselling.

'I have probably been very close to a complete breakdown on numerous occasions, when all sorts of grief and all sorts of lies and misconceptions and everything are coming to you from every angle,' he said.

It is wonderful that through the work of people like Ruby and Prince Harry the stigma around mental health issues is beginning to break down and we're beginning to see mental health as no different from physical health issues. And some mental health issues can be as disabling as serious physical health issues, although they're not obvious on the outside.

As Ruby puts it, 'The thing about depression is – and why people feel ... well I feel – a lot of shame is that there is nothing wrong with you on the outside. I mean you know you don't have any lumps, or you don't have any scars. You are not in a wheelchair. So people go "Come on, come on! Snap out of it. Cheer up ..." And that's really ludicrous and makes everything much worse – because you can't.

'It's not like you're sitting on your porch singing the blues with a banjo because your baby has left you. This is deep, dark, numbing abyss hell. You'll know when you have got it, but nobody will believe you – and that adds horror to it all.'

Having discovered mindfulness on a course with Michael and then gone on to complete a master's degree in mindfulness-based cognitive therapy at Oxford University, Ruby uses practices such as the ones we have shared to help her manage her own depression.

These days Ruby advises people to learn such practices to help them build their own defences against depression and anxiety. It can help them stop their own sadness, fear, guilt or self-criticism from building to a point where it becomes chronic and embedded.

The Mind Time practices we've shared can help develop our awareness of the stream of thoughts and feelings we experience. They also help us to see how we can become entangled in that stream in ways that aren't helpful. By witnessing this and by stepping out of that stream and onto the bank, even for a moment or two, we can begin to see familiar patterns in the flow of our thoughts and feelings.

Gradually, we can train ourselves to notice when those thoughts are taking over. We can begin to see and realise that those thoughts are simply 'mental events'. They come, they go, and they don't have to control us.

Most of us have issues that we find hard to let go. The practices we've shared can help us to deal with them more productively. We can ask ourselves questions such as, 'Is trying to solve this by brooding about it helpful, or am I just getting caught up in my thoughts?'

That can help us to notice signs of stress or anxiety earlier. And that helps us deal with these better. For some of us, doing practices like these when we're anxious or feeling low and self-critical is particularly difficult. At such times, when we stop what we're doing, thoughts and worries can crowd in. Remember, the practices aren't about making these thoughts go away. Rather, it's about seeing them as mental events.

So, if we find ourselves anxious and worrying about events at work, for example, maybe concerned about a meeting we're scheduled to have tomorrow and we keep worrying about how it's going to go and whether we'll remember to bring up all the points we think we need to raise, first we can prepare.

We can write things down, talk to a friend or colleague and get ourselves ready. Then, AIM to put it aside. Every time we find ourselves thinking about the meeting, we can notice and allow the feelings of anxiety that may come with that. We can use our developing meta-awareness to see that the thoughts and feelings that come are just thoughts, just feelings. We can perhaps let them be like leaves on a river, floating downstream while we stand on the bank watching. Sometimes we can be repeatedly drawn into the drama of our thinking and feeling. It can seem that it's too hard to let go. It can be as if we're pulled into the stream and all we can feel is the hard press of water as our thoughts and feelings press against us. Allowing that, letting it be, we can remember that whatever our thoughts tell us, in the end these are always only ever thoughts and feelings. They're just thoughts. Just feelings.

Some people find that it is easier to cope with an over-busy mind by doing exercises like gentle yoga, Pilates, tai chi or going for a walk. However we do it, it can be helpful to gently work at coming away from those unhelpful patterns of thinking and feeling – and seeing them for what they are: just patterns of thinking and feeling – over and over.

To develop their awareness of thoughts and feelings, some people find it helpful to silently name and allow them. 'Oh yes – here's the thought that I might lose my job.' Or, 'This is anxiety talking.' You're not fighting the thought, and the allowing attitude helps you stand back a little and just notice – just witness.

Some people find that it's especially helpful to develop meta-awareness and allowing when they realise that, for several minutes, they have been caught up in reliving past problems or pre-living future worries. At such times, we might find something here and now that can catch our curiosity; some embodied, present-moment experience we can get interested in.

AIM can calm our anxious minds and soothe our harsh self-criticism. But it takes time and it needs to be developed through practice. So if you're struggling with your thoughts and feelings, take the time to practise. And be patient. Gradually, bit by bit, your ability to AIM will improve.

That said, we strongly recommend that you seek advice from a GP or mental health professional if you are struggling with persistent low mood and anxiety.

KEY MESSAGES IN CHAPTER 6

- If you're not currently active, get moving. You can use AIM to help with this and you can begin to use your daily exercise routine as a way of strengthening your AIM.
- Most of us need more sleep. If you're falling asleep during Mind Time, you probably need more sleep. If you find yourself in the in-between state, between sleeping and waking, when you meditate, that can be helpful. Becoming more familiar with it, you can use it to generate ideas and to fall asleep more easily at night. AIM can help us to get to sleep when we're struggling at 4 a.m. It's especially helpful to use meta-awareness to see that any anxious thoughts and feelings at such times are just thoughts, just feelings. And it's really useful to make a more deliberate connection with your body to help you calm your mind and fall asleep.
- Many of us eat too much, and that's bad for our health. AIM can help us to savour our food and to notice whether we really do need to keep eating or whether we've had enough. It can connect us with our natural self-regulating mechanisms around what we eat.
- More and more people are speaking out about their mental health issues, and that's helping to de-stigmatise the issue. If you're prone to depressive rumination or anxious thoughts and feelings, AIM can help you to let go of these. Remember – in the end, however much they insist otherwise, your thoughts, your feelings are all just thoughts, just feelings.
- Taking 10 minutes for Mind Time every day is good for your health – body and mind.

Chapter 7

AIM for Better Work–Life Balance

ALL NIGHT LONG

When I (Megan) started work I joined a management consultancy firm in London. Often, my colleagues and I pulled an all-nighter – working all day, then through the night and into the next day too. I didn't mind that at all. In fact I enjoyed it. My work colleagues were my main social network. We had fun together. I was in my 20s, single, full of energy, with no other commitments to speak of. Work was the biggest part of my life and I thought working hard was exciting and cool. Glamorous even! I certainly didn't give the idea 'work–life balance' much thought.

Fast-forward 20 years. Now I'm a wife and the mother of two little girls. A few months ago, work took me to France for a couple of days. One evening, between courses at dinner with a client, I nipped out to make a quick call home. I got through to my husband, who sounded anxious. In the background, I could hear Lottie, my younger one, was sobbing. There was a pain in her stomach and we didn't know the cause. My heart froze and my stomach clenched.

There I was, far from home, half-crippled with concern, outside a restaurant with a client inside wondering what on earth had happened to me. iPad balanced precariously on my lap, I frantically Googled 'children pain in stomach', all the while harangued by inner voices lecturing me: I was a rubbish mother; I was letting my client down; I should be able to manage work and parenting better – and preferably at the same time.

At that moment, work and life felt extremely unbalanced.

Pulled in two different directions, I wondered how I could ever meet the needs of those around me – let alone my own. Acutely aware of what mattered most – my family – I also saw that my love and concern for them couldn't translate into 'I need to give up work altogether to be with them all the time'. I'm the main breadwinner and my work adds meaning and purpose to my life in the family.

Thankfully Lottie was absolutely fine, but my mixed emotions about balancing priorities between home and work are typical of what many of us experience.

○ HOW 'BALANCED' ARE YOU?

On a scale of 1 to 10, where 1 is strongly disagree and 10 is strongly agree, rate how you respond to these statements:

1. The way I navigate my work and non-work commitments matches what I know to be important to me.
2. I feel I am in control of the boundaries between my work life and my non-work life.
3. My non-work life isn't frequently interrupted by my work life – or if it is, I am at ease with that.
4. My work life isn't frequently interrupted by my non-work life – or if it is, I am at ease with that.
5. Do I first identify with my role(s) outside work or my role inside work? I am satisfied with my answer to this.
6. I feel I have sufficient time for myself.

How did you score on these questions? Were you above 7 or 8 on all the questions? That would indicate, on these criteria at least, that you are broadly satisfied with your work–life balance. Or are you reflecting on your low scores? That would suggest that you might be less satisfied, less at ease with how you 'balance' your work and non-work lives.

If you're in the second group, you're not alone. According to a study conducted by the Mental Health Foundation, a UK charity, a third of us feel unhappy or very unhappy about the time we devote to work.[1] And women are significantly more likely to fall into this group, probably because of the tensions and social expectations around being a mother as well as a worker.

This chapter, used alongside the Mind Time practices which develop AIM, is all about helping you to work out what sort of work–life balance will enable you to achieve what you want in life. It is also about supporting you to make clearer, more informed choices in how you navigate your work and non-work commitments. The phrase 'work–life balance' is often used to talk about the amount of time we spend at work compared with the amount of time we have outside it, but as Megan's story above shows, it seems far from a straightforward equation. There are factors apart from time to think about when we consider our own work–life balance.

⏱ WHAT DOES 'BALANCE' MEAN TO YOU?

When you think of your own work–life balance:

1. How much control do you have over when, where and how you work?
2. What stage of life are you at?
3. What commitments do you have outside work?
4. What support do you get outside work (for example with looking after elderly relatives or child-care)?
5. What is your pattern of work? Do you have gaps between different jobs?
6. How do you describe yourself? How would you want others to describe you?
7. What fulfils you? What is a meaningful life?

When we start to address the questions like those in the box above, it turns out that the phrase 'work–life balance' may be rather unhelpful. It's odd to separate 'work' and 'life' in this way, as if work isn't part of life and life isn't part of work. The idea of balance conjures up the image of weighing-scales, work on one side, life on the other, as if we simply need both somehow to be equal and balance each other out.

But it's not like that. For example:

- Maybe you work a lot, but you're in charge of when and where you do that and you figure your work–life balance isn't too bad.
- Or maybe you're young, single and without too many commitments. That might give you a different perspective on your work and life than if you are a single parent, or someone nearing retirement.

- Perhaps you think that the appalling hours you put into work this week are fine because you know you'll be stopping work for a while in a few months – maybe taking a career break.
- And if you're among the lucky few who adore what they do at work and find it meaningful, then tipping the scales towards 'work' might be pretty good; whereas if you're thoroughly disengaged with your work, it's absolutely not good.

Working out what work–life balance means for us is vital in living a fulfilling and productive life. But it can be a rather tricky exercise.

AIM can help. Practising Mind Time every day enables us to turn down the volume on the critical self-talk that can so often kick off in work–life conflicts. This allows us to be more compassionate towards ourselves as we navigate what are often very complex questions of prioritisation.

Has your Mind Time practice slipped?

If you've not been doing it for a while, just start again.

Remember – you never blow it. It's always there to pick up again.

AIM helps us to open space for inquiry, helping us to ask questions about our experiences and engage deeply with what is meaningful to us. They help us develop our ability to tune into our bodies and minds, and that gives us clues as to when we are 'in balance' or swerving significantly off course.

Let's look at these in more depth by starting with some inquiry. If we don't know what it is that we want from life and what makes it meaningful, then it is tricky to prioritise what we do every day.

Here are some questions we can carefully inquire into, bringing to them the warm and compassionate focus that AIM develops.

WHAT DO I WANT TO DO WITH MY LIFE?

'Tell me, what is it you want to do with your one wild and precious life?' asks Mary Oliver, in her poem 'A Summer Day'.

What would you say right now if you were asked and you just had to respond immediately?

Some of us have our answer to hand. Others of us may have intended to think this stuff through at some point, but found that the weeks, months and years went by and we didn't give these questions the attention they deserve.

But if we don't think about what's important to us, it's likely that we'll just go on ping-ponging between work and life commitments. That can leave us plagued with feelings of dissatisfaction and a nagging sense that we're making the wrong choices or missing opportunities.

Vivienne, a friend of mine (Megan's), came to see me one day with a problem. She had a persistent sense of unease about her job along with distressing feelings of guilt about the amount of time she spent doing it. She told me that six years ago she'd promised herself that she would reassess what she was doing and change her work so that she had more time with her family. But those six years whizzed by and she still couldn't say why she was working such long hours and compromising her time at home.

Many of us find ourselves in similar situations, maybe because it's scary to think more deeply about what's important. If we do that, we may feel that we have wasted time. Or it might turn out that we must make even scarier decisions and implement real changes in our lives.

But wouldn't that be better than sticking our head in the sand and hoping things will somehow change by themselves?

With AIM – allowing, inquiry and meta-awareness – we can face up to and navigate tough questions and then respond to them more compassionately and authentically.

Inquiring about my purpose

Regularly inquiring into what is important in our lives is like remembering to set our compass when we are navigating at sea. We wouldn't think of getting on a boat – especially if we have others we care about alongside us – and allowing the sea and the wind to take us wherever, hoping that somehow we might just end up on a nice beach.

But sometimes that's what we do with our lives. We can get stuck on automatic pilot, passively allowing the changing circumstances of the world around us to dictate our decisions. As a result, we can come to feel trapped in a pattern of 'work' and 'life' that we don't want.

By giving us the tools to come out of automatic pilot, AIM is a bit like giving us access to a compass so that we can check our direction regularly. Rather than leaving it to chance to see where we end up, we find we are able to make *conscious choices* that consider our needs and the needs of those who are accompanying us on our journey.

Through helping to AIM, it is possible to figure out and face up to what is important to us. It is possible to prioritise day-to-day what we commit to, as well as to make longer-term important decisions about our careers and personal lives.

Here's a technique that we use to help in this process. It can help you to start thinking about your own work–life balance.

⏱ WRITING A LETTER HOME

Imagine yourself in the future sometime – it might be in 2, 5 or 10 years' time, or even when you're 80 or 90 years old – however long ahead that is for you. Just choose a timeframe that feels right.

Imagine that at that point in time you are living a purposeful, meaningful life.

Then imagine that the future you which you have envisaged is writing a letter to you today, describing their life.

Using the present tense, consider some of the following questions as you write your letter:

Self-image: Since the future you, who is now writing this letter, is exactly the kind of person you want to be, living that imagined purposeful and meaningful life, what are your qualities? What is your attitude to life? How are you feeling?

Personal impact: What do others say about you? How do your work colleagues describe you? How do your friends and family describe you?

Work: What is your work situation? What impact are you having? What are you contributing towards?

Personal learning: How are you approaching your own learning and development?

Community: How are you influencing the culture and community around you?

Home: What is your living environment?

Health: How is your health, fitness and anything else to do with your body?

Relationships: What type of relationship do you have with your colleagues, your family and your friends?

Other: What else are you doing? What else do you have? What else do you give to others? How do you feel?

As you are writing this letter, here are a few pointers that might help make it come to life and feel more attainable:

- It is difficult to create a personal vision that relies on *someone else* changing. For example, saying: *'My work colleagues are all kind and considerate'* probably won't change your colleagues in the least! It might be better to focus on what *you* can influence.
- It can help to focus on what you want to move towards rather than what you want to avoid. For example, rather than saying: *'I have given up fast food and my sedentary lifestyle,'* you could say: *'I am a healthy person, enjoying exercise.'*
- Tension and movement can be created when you say: *'I am feeling fulfilled in my work,'* but not when you say: *'In two years' time I will feel fulfilled in my work.'*
- If you struggle with knowing what you might want to be doing and experiencing, try thinking back to significant and meaningful experiences you have had – times when you have felt a sense of fulfilment. Exploring these may help you discover what your core values are.
- Decide what you want for yourself rather than setting a goal to be better than somebody else. You can look at, and learn from, the example other people set. But then translate it into something that is right for you.
- The clearer the picture is to you, the stronger it will be. Having said that, you don't need to know now exactly what job you will be in or where you will live – just be specific about the qualities of your work and your home. You don't need to know when you will retire – just consider how you will transition.
- It is good to think of an imagined future that is both personally stretching *and* achievable.

After doing the exercise above, you might have a better idea about what is most important to you. Inquiring and regularly asking yourself questions about the sort of person you want to be and the kind of impact you want to be having on others is fundamental in helping you to prioritise your work and your non-work. Knowing that we have done this sort of inquiry and will be revisiting it again soon helps us as we go about trying to juggle our commitments.

CAN WE REALLY 'HAVE IT ALL'?

We were recently invited to take part in a panel discussion for people whose work lives were hugely demanding. The theme was 'Can we really have it all?' The panel were debating, among themselves and with the audience, whether we must simply accept that there is a trade-off between high performance and work–life balance. The assumption in the room was that if we want to succeed at 'work' we'll need to sacrifice a great deal of 'life'.

The discussion was fascinating and highlighted one of the most simplistic and embedded myths of our time: the more we work, the more we achieve. This assumption has serious consequences for work–life balance, and it drives many of us to work very hard.

But how true is it?

If you had to argue the case either for or against the assumption, what would you say?

Take a look at the Pressure–Performance Curve shown opposite.

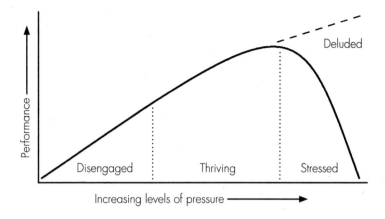

This model illustrates an age-old relationship between levels of pressure and corresponding performance.[2] At first, as pressure or levels of challenge increase, our performance rises. We have all experienced this. If we are ever given a job that we could do almost in our sleep, after a while we grow bored or apathetic in the face of too simple a task. We become disengaged and our performance suffers. But when we're given a job where the level of interest and challenge feel just 'right' – challenging but still manageable – we rise to the occasion and our performance increases.

But those performance improvements don't continue indefinitely. At some point the pressure increases to the level where we become stressed. And at that point our performance begins to decline.

Here's the important issue though: we may not realise that we have reached that point.

Many of us, convinced that if we work harder we'll produce more and perform better, ignore the 'life' bit of work–life balance and put our heads down and try harder. When we do that we can find ourselves saying things like the comments in the illustration overleaf. Do any of them sound familiar? Of course, comments like these might be fine in some circumstances. As we said, work–life balance is a matter for the individual and we are all different. Each

of us has our own particular pressure–performance curve – and this can change over time. Some of us retain higher levels of performance at higher levels of pressure than others. But if we find ourselves saying these sorts of things habitually, and if we are also noticing signs of exhaustion, then we may have entered the 'zone of delusion'.

In the zone of delusion, we think that by continuing to tip the balance away from 'life' and towards 'work' we're performing well and getting things done. But we're not. And most people around us can probably tell. We work harder and harder, believing it will help us out of this current busyness and that it's just temporary. Instead we find ourselves in a vicious cycle of more and more work and less and less 'life'.

If this happens we may be on the edge of burnout and in danger of entering what's known as the Exhaustion Funnel, and we need to find a way out.

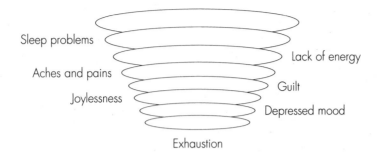

Sleep problems
Lack of energy
Aches and pains
Guilt
Joylessness
Depressed mood
Exhaustion

Exhaustion

The diagram above shows the Exhaustion Funnel developed by Marie Asberg, a clinical professor who specialises in burnout.

HAVE YOU ENTERED THE EXHAUSTION FUNNEL?

Do you *frequently* experience any or many of the things below?

- Wake up in the morning and notice that your body is aching – perhaps your shoulders/neck/back?
- Feel tired, frequently, both at work and outside work?
- Find it difficult to get to sleep or wake up regularly with many thoughts running through your mind?
- Feel guilty when you are at work about not being elsewhere (e.g. with the children, or with an elderly parent)?
- Feel guilty when not at work that you should be working?
- Find it tricky to remember more than one or two moments of joy in your day?
- Feel depressed, not wanting to get up in the morning?

Symptoms such as those mentioned can point to exhaustion and signal a need to protect our physical and mental well-being.

To do this, we need to uncover delusion – and AIM helps us with that.

Uncovering delusion

With meta-awareness of our thoughts, feelings, sensations and impulses, we're able to notice more frequently when we tip over the top of the performance curve and into the zone of delusion. The practices in this book help us to habitually check in with how we are. We are more likely to notice when we are trying to convince ourselves that we're fine and we just have to carry on. We are more likely to notice when our body and mind give us clues that we're entering the Exhaustion Funnel.

Many of the people who have been practising Mind Time and using AIM tell us that they feel more connected to their bodies and are able to pay more attention to pain and tension. Although that might sound like something we would rather ignore, if we notice these things early we can do something about them – preventing a situation where our body and mind have got themselves into a more serious, even irreversible condition where we need medical help.

It is when we notice that we are deluded that we have to stick up for ourselves and respect our boundaries more.

How do you manage the boundaries between 'work' and 'life'? Can you 'switch off' from work if and when you need to? For some of us, the blurring of boundaries can deepen the Exhaustion Funnel; for others it gives us freedom to do what we want, when we want to.

Either way, AIM helps us to make clearer choices about our boundaries, which can, in turn, help us to stay on top of the curve.

Disappearing work–life boundaries

The more hours you spend at work, the more hours away from work you are likely to spend thinking or worrying about it. As a typical person's weekly working hours increase, so do their feelings of unhappiness.[3]

Smartphones allow us the opportunity to be connected to work for longer. For some of us that gives us freedom. For others, it means our 'life' is being invaded.

HOW DEPENDENT ARE YOU ON YOUR DEVICES?

When do you first check your phone in the day? Do you sneak a quick look as soon as your alarm (which is on your phone) goes off?

A third of us check our phones within five minutes of waking up.

How often do you check your phone, do you think? Once an hour? Every five minutes?

In the UK collectively, smartphone users check their phones more than one billion times a day.[4]

When do you check your phone? Are there any moments that are 'off-limits' for you?

An enormous 80 per cent of us use our smartphone while having a conversation with friends, and two-thirds of us are on our phones during the family dinner. Some of us can't even leave them alone while we're trying to sleep – a third of us check them in the middle of the night.[5]

If you added up the amount of time you put into checking email on your phone, how much would it add up to?

One study found that workers checking for new email added as much as 2 hours to their working day.[6]

When you're on holiday, do you leave work entirely at home?

TripAdvisor, the online travel site, claims that most people now check work email on holiday and make calls back to the office.[7]

Being 'always on' and always connected can bring us some freedom. It can help some of us choose when and where we work. More and more of us want this freedom: those born after 1980 are likely to believe that they should have the ability to set their own work patterns. They're also more likely to blur the lines between work and home.[8] This freedom might also be important to people such as parents, whose child-care commitments mean they want to stop work in the afternoon to pick their kids up from school, or for those caring for elderly relatives who need to visit them during the day. Employers sometimes allow this on the understanding that the laptop comes out again in the evening.

But for many of us the physical and psychological blurring of the boundary between 'work' and 'life' is tricky to navigate. Far from giving us more control, many of us feel we have less.

How do *you* feel you manage your work–life boundaries? Perhaps you choose to separate both as far as possible. Perhaps you prefer to integrate and constantly bounce back and forth between work and 'life' activities.

One important question in all of this is whether we feel we still have *choice* in our approach. This is where another link with AIM comes in. When AIM is practised over and over in Mind Time, we open up a space where we are able to choose our response rather than react in automatic patterns.

It's not that one of the strategies above is better than the other. But if we AIM to give ourselves choice and take some kind of control over which strategy we use, then we'll begin to feel more on top of things – and that helps us to flourish.

META-AWARENESS – OPENING CHOICE AT THE WORK–LIFE BOUNDARY

When we are able to notice that our thoughts are galloping into the future or ruminating in the past and then bring our attention into the present moment, we can become more aware of the choices we have, right now. We can actively choose what to do, right now.

Jon – an old friend of Megan's – has the wonderful ability to be both straight-talking and kind. Despite that, he struggles with managing the boundaries between work and family life and feels that he does neither of his key roles – being a self-employed accountant and being a father of three – well. Through working with practices such as those in this book, he gradually managed to catch himself and make choices about paying attention fully to one role or the other, rather than blurring them and pretending multitasking works.

This is what he said to us:

'I had a really important turning point with one of my children. One bedtime Rosie, who was having trouble with her friendships at school, asked me to put her to bed. I had work to do – in fact I was facing quite a backlog of stuff, so I was working on my laptop at home. I said, "Oh, I've got a report to finish, love. Mum's going to put you to bed tonight." But she really wanted me to do it. Luckily, out of the corner of my eye, I just briefly caught that tiny glimpse of disappointment on her face. I realised that in that moment I had a choice. A few seconds later, I closed the laptop. She needed me, she was asking for me. I went up and put her to bed. We talked through her worries and what she could do. She looked much more settled. When I went back downstairs I still had to do the report for work – but now I could wholeheartedly and efficiently focus on it rather than struggling with the knowledge that I didn't do the right thing. Funnily enough, I probably completed it all quicker.'

Like Jon, many of us spend far too long half-heartedly working on one thing, getting distracted with another thing, then trying to go back to the first thing. We end up multitasking and doing nothing well. Jon felt he was neither doing his best with his work nor with his children when he was mixing these two roles together.

Part of the solution to concerns about work–life balance lies in giving our full attention to work when at work, and then giving our full attention to our activities outside work when we are outside work. That way, the quality of what we do in both goes up.

To that end, some degree of separation can be beneficial. Adam, who works long, hard hours in the UK National Health Service, has also been working with the Mind Time practices in this book. He told us that he now habitually pauses for a moment as he puts the key into the keyhole of his front door at the end of his working day. He said that before he began working more consciously with his mind, he was unaware of how much he brought the often stressful and negative emotions from work into the house. His family often 'caught' these emotions from him and, before he knew it, the whole household was in a foul mood!

Now he specifically inquires, as the key goes in, 'What sort of mood do I want to bring into my family?' 'What impact do I want to have on those I love this evening?' 'What do I want them to "catch" from me?'

Through practising AIM he is now able to take a few crucial breaths and acknowledge to himself what mood he is in. He then opens up the possibility for changing his mood and the moods of those he loves.

Some of us can rejuvenate by carefully protecting the boundary between 'work' and 'life' and wholeheartedly enjoying our non work activities. But many of us face greater challenges outside work than in it.

INCREASING PRESSURES OUTSIDE WORK

For some of us, our time outside work is a time when we can focus on what we enjoy – hobbies, exercise, reading and seeing friends and family.

Many of us, though, have commitments outside work, which mean we can't do exactly as we please. We may enjoy these commitments or we may feel stressed and overwhelmed by them. Sometimes we carry a heavy sense of obligation.

Judy, a very talented colleague of ours, has more respite at work than at home at the moment. She's a single parent with two young children. Her father died last year and her mother is suffering from dementia. Her brother lives several hours away. Her mother is in and out of hospital and, as we write, a solution hasn't been found for her care. There is a mound of administrative duties tied up with the process of linking her into social services.

Recovery time is something that Judy needs to find fast, but she faces more pressure outside than inside work.

More and more of us are called upon to care for an elderly relative, an ill partner or a disabled child.[9,10] It's especially tough for single parents – and more and more of us find ourselves needing to bring up our kids single-handedly.[11] Then there are issues like educational courses we may engage in, and the charities, churches or community groups that pull on our time. All of this means that we often don't have much time for relaxing and rejuvenating activities. And that means we really have to do what Judy has done successfully with the help of AIM, which is understanding and calling in our lifelines.

LIFELINES

'Lifelines' are activities that nourish and resource us. They might include things like going for a walk outside in nature, meeting up with friends, listening to music or having a hot bubble bath. We each have different things that relax and rejuvenate us. What we can do, when we feel signs of exhaustion through work or non-work commitments, is to reach out to these lifelines and do more of them.

Unfortunately, what many of us do is the polar opposite: we 'battle on'. We gradually cut down on nourishing activities – the circles in the Exhaustion Funnel gradually narrow, indicating how our lives narrow to just doing the things we think are urgent – and our stress levels increase. In this way we make a fundamental, false assumption: we think these lifelines are optional.

They aren't.

We might be able to get away with skipping them for a short period of time, but after a while, if we continue to exhaust ourselves, we can suffer very real physical and mental problems that can be difficult for us to recover from. Sometimes we keep going until we get a very rude wake-up call.

Take Simon. We met him at the 'can we have it all' event described above (*see page 152*). Four years ago, Simon was working at a law firm in the City. Committed to his career, he had a senior position and worked long hours at a fast pace. One morning he left for work, as usual, very early at 6 a.m., to be at his desk for 7 a.m. Walking to the train station on a dark and wet November morning through deserted streets in North London, he suddenly felt his chest tighten. He initially thought it was indigestion but the pain worsened. With nobody around to help him, he turned round and somehow made it back home. When his wife opened the door he collapsed through it. By 7.30 a.m. he was on the operating table. He had had a major heart attack – at the age of 44.

He was off work for seven months. He was diagnosed as diabetic and this, along with the stressful work life, contributed to his heart attack.

While he was off work he had plenty of time to think about how he was looking after himself and what it was that was *really* most important to him in life. He is now back at work at the same law firm, but he works fewer hours and from home two days a week. He has radically changed his diet and alcohol intake and does more exercise. He now feels he has a healthier relationship with his work and his non-work life: 'I don't take work quite so seriously now – there are other things in life.'

He is reticent to give others advice about how they should approach their work–life balance, but one thing he was keen to suggest is that it is critical to think deeply about what is *actually* important to you.

It is difficult to ignore things if you find yourself having a heart attack aged 44. But for most of us, it is all too easy to ignore warning signs and assume it will be OK in the end. Sometimes it's all about surviving the week. We neglect the lifelines that can make us more resilient to physical and mental health problems. This situation is unsustainable – it does us no good and therefore it is not helping those we love either.

Spotting that your lifelines have slipped

When we have developed our capacity to AIM through Mind Time, when we're more alive to each moment, then we're also more aware of our lifelines – and we appreciate them more. There are two parts to this.

First, we can choose, in the moment, to prioritise activities that give us energy and bolster our resilience. By paying attention to our mind and body we are able to discern which activities give us a sense of joy and relaxation. Some of these activities might be very obvious to us – for example, we might know that playing music helps us to unwind. But some activities might be fleeting and seemingly mundane, such as those three minutes when we walk through nature from where our car is parked to our workplace. Those five minutes when we have a quick catch-up with a really good friend. The delicious coffee that we buy most mornings – but tend to drink in a rush. (Think back to Chapter 4, where we discuss how we can become more aware of these sorts of activities, in our average day, which build us up and give us strength and joy.)

Second, once we have identified these activities, we can learn to savour these lifelines (even if they are few and far between) when we are experiencing them, so we really make the most of those perhaps rare occasions when we are more relaxed in the moment and able to enjoy that.

When I (Megan) first did the *Nourish Yourself* exercise in Chapter 4 (*see page 93*) and thought about the activities that nourish me, I noticed that I was missing out on the full benefit of a particularly special five-minute period every morning. Every morning, my two girls come into my bed for five minutes while I have a cup of tea. They snuggle in and play with their toys. As I thought about this small moment I realised that my mind was often on the day ahead – quickly running through my to-do list and consequently getting stressed, determined or thoughtful, depending on what I felt the day ahead held in store.

I realised that this time with my two girls was incredibly precious and could be a bit like plugging myself into a battery, which gave me energy and joy for the day. Besides, I achieved absolutely nothing by running through my to-do list yet again during these five minutes. So I decided, using AIM, to focus wholeheartedly on my experience of snuggling up with my girls. Now, in those five minutes, my mood lifts, I reconnect with what is important and head into the day in a different way. It's a lifeline for me and might well be for them too – especially now that they can sense their mother is totally present with them.

ALLOWING – BEING 'GOOD ENOUGH'

AIM helps us to question our assumptions around our work–life balance and to spot when we feel 'unbalanced'. We become better able to discern and prioritise the activities which resource and nourish us, and that helps us to be more productive at work and to get the most out of those times when we are not at work.

It also helps us to allow and accept that, despite using all the tools above, the perfect work–life balance may just be too tricky to perpetually sustain.

Life is often not quite as accommodating as we want it to be. Our ideal work–life balance is wrenched out of the ground by something that happens. Our best intentions to go to the gym this week are overturned by an event at work, which just *has* to be prioritised. We become ill and this pulls down our ability to perform at work and in our other roles. We feel mortified that we forgot the kids' dress-up day at school because we were thinking only about the extra shift we had to do at work …

Allowing is about being 'good enough'. It is about understanding that we are human beings and we can't control the external environment, but we can influence our response to it. It is understanding that sometimes our best intentions to balance and prioritise don't play out, but knowing that we can pause, get things back in perspective and reset things again. In short, allowing is about caring for ourselves and those around us.

Think about the last time your intentions were thwarted. Perhaps you had decided to visit your elderly relative but were then asked by someone at work to fix something urgently for them. Perhaps you promised to do a report for your work but then your child was ill and you had to stay home. Can you remember how you reacted? What did that internal voice say to you? Perhaps it was rather judgemental: 'This is a disaster! I'm so rubbish at this! I never manage to keep my promises – I'm just not a very good mother/ father/daughter/work colleague.' Or perhaps it was more allowing and said something gentle and calming like, 'Oh well, these things happen. What can I do to make the best of the situation?'

As well as allowing for the fact that sometimes we will find ourselves in situations where we feel we don't have much choice in what we do, the attitude of allowing we learn during Mind Time is also directed towards others.

When someone demands that we re-do some work which we know will take all weekend, or when our partner demands that we spend some time this weekend doing some DIY that is rather overdue, our internal voice may begin to wish that the other person or the circumstances were different. If we find ourselves stuck with that voice repeating our wish over and over it doesn't tend to help the situation; it wears us down and we have no space to think more creatively or to turn our attention towards the other person's needs.

Without letting others walk all over us, it is possible to be more kind and accepting towards others and their requests. It may well be that we decide to refuse their demand this time round – but if we are allowing, we are more likely to communicate that in a way that protects our relationship with them. We know that people who have worked with AIM become more able to empathise. Allowing has a big part to play in this. It helps us to see things from the other person's perspective, not simply from within our own frame of reference.

Do keep going with Mind Time.

Just 10 minutes a day can really improve your AIM.

AIM FOR BETTER WORK–LIFE BALANCE

AIM helps us to negotiate our commitments better inside and outside work. We allow ourselves to be 'good enough', accepting that things will always happen that unsettle our sense of balance. We inquire into our purpose, about what gives us meaning in life, and about how we can make potentially difficult decisions in prioritising. We develop meta-awareness around how we choose, experience and stick to our work–life boundaries in the moment, and how we figure out what our lifelines are.

If practising 10 minutes every day makes it more likely that we will find ourselves satisfied with the decisions we have made in our life, then it is surely time very well spent.

KEY MESSAGES IN CHAPTER 7

- Work–life balance is more complex than a simple equation.
- Using AIM we can inquire about our purpose and what is meaningful to us. That helps us to navigate pressure – we have a compass to guide us.
- As we perceive pressure to be increasing, after a certain point our performance starts to fall. The pressure-performance curve shows how we enter the 'delusion zone' and can move into an 'exhaustion funnel'.
- By tuning in more to our present-moment experience by being meta-aware of our thoughts, feelings and sensations, we can notice when we get to this point.
- Flexible working and technological advances in communication mean our work–life boundaries are blurring – we are always 'on'. AIM helps us to actively choose where we set our own boundaries.
- Many of us face increasing pressure outside work due to commitments such as caring for others. However, by developing our AIM and allowing and accepting that our 'balance' is bound to get upset – that's just life – we can be more compassionate with others and ourselves. We can encourage a more supportive internal voice and stay in a more resourceful state.

Chapter 8

AIMing When Times Are Tough

Every one of us experiences hard times. Life can seem harsh and even cruel in these moments. AIM can help us find a more resourceful way of being with the things we can't easily change.

SUFFERING CHANGE

Vidyamala Burch, a good friend of Michael's, has a paralysed bladder and bowel.[1] She is partially paraplegic and experiences chronic severe pain. It's like a toothache in the spine and down her legs, she says, accompanied by a grinding joint pain in her back and feet.

Ask her to describe her quality of life and, with a broad, open smile, she'll tell you that she's flourishing.

But it wasn't always like that.

Born in New Zealand, Vidyamala loved hill-walking and rock-climbing – especially in New Zealand's stunning Southern Alps. But, aged 16, while lifting someone out of a pool during life-saving practice, she injured her spine. The major surgery that followed marked the start of a life of chronic pain. In just a few months she went from being a happy, sporty person to becoming more and more withdrawn, losing any sense that her body was a pleasant place to be. Seven years later, as a passenger in a car whose driver fell asleep at the wheel, she had another accident and a spinal fracture. There was more hospitalisation, more surgery. Ever since then her pain has been severe.

At the time of the second accident she was working as a film editor, hugely driven, putting in 60 hours a week at the editing desk. She now speaks of that period as a time of denial. Running away from herself, trying to escape her situation by pushing on through the pain, she tried to live her life as normally as possible.

The strain of that led to a physical breakdown and she ended up in hospital for three weeks. Her treatment there led to a raft of complications and the situation seemed to get worse and worse.

One night in the hospital, filled with fear, she had a life-changing experience. Unable to lie down to sleep for 24 hours because of her treatment, sitting up straight in her hospital bed propped with pillows, she had a night of acute crisis.

'It was like I had two different voices in my head. The determined part of myself was insisting that I could get through this ordeal. The other part of me, maybe the more realistic side, was completely vulnerable and kept saying that I couldn't cope and that there was no way I would get through to the morning.

'Then it was as though a third voice came through the darkness with a strong message that was telling me I didn't have to get through to morning, all I needed to do was get through this next moment.'

Immediately she went from feeling stressed and desperate to feeling almost relaxed, even confident. She saw that it was possible to live this moment. By changing her perspective, by stopping agonising about future torment to simply resting in each present moment, she got through that night.

The experience left her completely changed. 'It was as though I had one life leading up to that moment and another life after it.'

Vidyamala realised that what she had done in her mind changed the experience in her body. Pain is *not* all in the mind, she says. If someone had told her that while she was struggling, she would have become angry. Clearly, her body was damaged and that was the inescapable source of her pain. But she learned that you can use your mind to regulate the pain. The mind can turn down the volume of the pain. Above all, you can learn to take a new perspective on your experience.

Having learned to meditate soon after leaving hospital more than 30 years ago, Vidyamala now runs Breathworks, an international training organisation dedicated to helping people manage chronic pain more effectively.

One of the keys to the Breathworks approach, an idea that we strongly share, is that suffering comes to us in two forms: primary and secondary.

TWO KINDS OF SUFFERING

Primary suffering, like the pain Vidyamala experiences, is inescapable. It's an unavoidable part of our being human that life will deliver the unwanted – time and time again. Pain, loss, illness, bereavement, grief. We can't avoid these. Secondary suffering, however, is a different matter. It directly follows from the unwise reactions we have to whatever primary suffering has occurred.

While she was working as a film editor, Vidyamala experienced constant pain. That was her primary suffering. But her unwillingness to allow that to be the case produced a huge amount of secondary suffering. She didn't want the pain to be there. But it was. Constantly wishing things were other than they actually were; struggling and tensing against the pain; pushing herself to keep going – all of these in themselves were producing different forms of secondary suffering. Now she had her pain – that was bad enough – *as well as* the secondary suffering that came from trying to deny the pain. And that, she eventually learned, was optional. Once she dropped her determined unwillingness to allow what is the case to be the case, her secondary suffering significantly decreased.

What this shows is that some of the unhappiness we all experience comes not so much from the unwanted events that come to us as from our unwise reactions to those events. We all want to be happy; none of us wants to suffer. But the way we go about trying to get rid of suffering in our lives often serves to increase it.

Just because we're human, some of the time we're bound to experience pain. But suffering – now that's a different story. Pain is inevitable; suffering is optional. Why? Because much of what we call suffering comes from our deep unwillingness to allow the pain we can't avoid.

Our choice, and our potential for freedom, lies in what follows the unwanted experience. We can be with it wisely, or unwisely. We can unwisely react, or wisely respond.

DON'T REACT, RESPOND

You're sitting in a railway carriage, on your way to a family gathering, and the train comes to an unexpected stop. After five minutes, people in the overcrowded carriage start to look around – why have we stopped? The driver makes an announcement: 'You're probably wondering why we're stopped here. I've just been informed that there's a track defect ahead and we need to go slow through this part of the system. But there are four trains ahead of us and one of them is the slow, stopping service. It seems that our journey will be delayed by another 35 minutes.'

You're going to miss part of the meal, but that's not the main thing. There are people there you see only rarely and some of that precious opportunity has now gone. You'll need to adjust your expectations. Look around the carriage, though. Your fellow passengers now divide into two categories: the unwise reactors and the wise responders.

The wise responders do what they can to limit the damage: they make calls, send emails or texts and do whatever they need to do to get things back into some kind of alignment in their day. Then they might read a book, listen to music, do some work, meditate or stare out the window. An extra 40 minutes can be a valuable piece of time in anyone's day.

The unwise reactors, on the other hand, are becoming increasingly upset and frustrated by what's happening. Brows are furrowing, jaws are clenching and blood pressure is rising. In a vain effort to rid themselves of the pain of frustration, some of the unwise reactors turn to one another and complain about the state of Britain's railways. Or they get on their phones and find someone else to rant to. Or they sit tutting to themselves, steaming and fidgeting, growing increasingly red, increasingly unhappy.

Allowing what is the case to be the case and then choosing what we're going to do next – that's a key part of learning to reduce secondary suffering. It's a key component in the quest for greater happiness.

> Do keep going with your Mind Time.
>
> And don't expect too much too soon.
>
> We've all had years of building other habits of mind.
>
> Change can take time.

BUILDING YOUR RESILIENCE

Of course, missing part of a family gathering sits fairly low on the scale of unwanted events. Some of what life deals us is very much more dramatic. More than half of us will experience severe trauma – a life-threatening event – at some point in our lives, and none of us is immune to life-changing challenges: the death of those we love, the loss of jobs or relationships, illness and physical accidents.[2]

It's an inescapable part of our being human that these things will come to us, and it's also a part of our being human that most of us will bounce back from them. We have what Ann Masten, who studies resilience, has called a kind of 'Ordinary Magic' – a natural capacity to recover from adversity.[3] In the face of severe trauma, a small proportion of us will experience mental ill health. Illnesses like Post-Traumatic Stress Disorder (PTSD) are slowly becoming better understood. But what's important about the magic of resilience is that there are things we can all do to actively build it when trauma occurs.

The American Psychological Association has identified 10 ways to build your personal resilience.[4] Here is our take on that, adapted to take AIM into account.

Ten steps to building personal resilience

1. Make connections
It's important that we keep up our relationships with close family members and good friends. For some of us, social, civic and faith groups are also helpful. Sometimes, if we can help others in their time of need, that can also help us. By allowing others to be who they are, we can allow them to help us too. Inquiring into their experience, we can let them inquire into ours.

For some people, their strongest connection might be with a pet or other animal. That can be hugely helpful.

Wherever our deepest connections lie, it can help to make a point of noticing our thoughts, feelings, sensations and impulses when we're with others. Sometimes, sharing these can help. In this way, AIM can help build stronger connections.

2. Avoid seeing crises as insurmountable problems
Stressful events happen. That's unavoidable. But with AIM we can change how we interpret and react to them. By letting what is the case be the case a bit more, noticing any tendency to build things up unnecessarily, AIM can help to get things into proportion.

3. Accept that change is a part of living
Circumstances change and we need to change with them. We can AIM to allow things to be as they actually are instead of fighting it or trying to deny what's actually going on. Allowing that there are some things that can't be changed can help us focus on what we can change.

4. Setting goals
If your goals are realistic, even small things done regularly can help us move towards them. We can use AIM to be realistic about

that. When we know that we're doing what we *can* do, perhaps we can more easily allow for the fact that we can't do everything.

5. Take decisive actions
AIM to act. Problems and stresses don't go away just because we wish they would. When we let what is the case be the case a bit more often, we can choose more readily what we're actually going to do – and then we can act.

6. Look for opportunities for self-discovery
We can learn so much from any struggle with loss. AIM can help us to allow the world and other people to be as they are. It helps us to inquire deeply into what we find. We can notice how changing circumstances impact on our own thoughts, feelings, sensations and impulses. As we learn more about the world, about others and about ourselves, our feelings of appreciation for this life can deepen.

7. Cultivate a positive self-view
AIM lends a new strength to face the challenges life brings. We allow what is the case to be the case, and treat ourselves and others with a bit more kindness. We inquire with curiosity and openness into what's actually going on in ourselves, others and the world around us. We step back ever so slightly and see with meta-awareness that our thoughts are just thoughts, our feelings are just feelings, our sensations are just passing sensations. When we do all of that then we can know 'I can be with this – I'm strong enough'.

8. Keep things in perspective
AIM to see that, however challenging our own circumstances, there's a big wide world out there. AIM can help you to keep a sense of perspective. It can open that small space where we react

a bit less, respond a bit more. That can help to keep things from blowing out of proportion.

9. Maintain a hopeful outlook
AIM to notice how unwanted events can set off negative trails of thinking and feeling. In the end, though, these are just thoughts, just feelings. We can notice the *quality* of our thinking and feeling at times of trouble. If those thoughts and feelings seem unduly negative, AIM can help us to see that they're just thoughts, just feelings. When we find that, we can experiment and see what it's like to shift our attention elsewhere.

10. Take care of yourself
Do things that you enjoy and find relaxing. Exercise regularly. Keep up your Mind Time practice – keep your AIM on track.

In all of this, the key is to identify ways that work well for us as we develop our strategies for building resilience. We can return to the list above and take each point in turn. To what extent are we already doing some of these things? How might we build further on any of the points listed? What would we enjoy doing more of? What might be a bit of a stretch or challenge to do more of?

On 'Make Connections', for example, some of us are naturally gregarious and love to spend time in social gatherings connecting with others. We get energy from that. Others of us are less extroverted – we like to spend time alone and find that naturally energising. The point here isn't to encourage those of us who are more introverted to change our nature and become extroverts – that would be simply stressful. Rather, it's important to recognise and build on our natural preferences. If we're gregarious, we can make the most of that and think about ways we could build on it. Are there clubs or social groups we've always meant to join but haven't? If we prefer our own company or spending time with just one or two special friends, we can try getting dates in our diary more frequently and keep our friendships in good repair.

It's great to know that, however resilient we already are, we can build on that and develop it still further. But the idea of resilience somehow implies the idea of coming back to a baseline, regaining the ground we had lost as a result of a challenge. It's possible to do better than that. Sometimes, even powerful and apparently cataclysmic challenges can be the opportunity for genuine growth. And the chances of that happening are significantly enhanced when we build in AIM – as we'll see in the next section.

BEYOND RESILIENCE

In Chapter 4 we saw there are simple things we can do to increase our positivity. But however much we seek out and savour the positive, our lives will always bring us things we want and things we don't. There's simply no avoiding that. But when dramatic changes occur, if you have developed the capacity for savouring the positive, and if you have developed the capacities of inquiry, allowing and meta-awareness, then those changes can turn out to be occasions for real growth and development.

Consider the story of Jacob. He is 63 and has been in hospital being treated for a potentially fatal cancer. His stay in hospital has been tough. He's been going through a debilitating series of surgical interventions, then chemotherapy and then radiotherapy. All of which have slowly ground his spirit down.

As part of his treatment, he has learned practices similar to the Mind Time ones we've shared.

One morning, lying in bed, he started to think about all that had happened since his cancer diagnosis. Projecting forward from that, he found himself overwhelmed by grim thoughts of his impending death. But instead of dwelling on these he chose to do one of the practices.

Allowing his thoughts to come and go, deliberately choosing not to suppress them, he began to see the thought 'My life is over – I'm doomed' as just a thought.

He noticed the enormous feelings of despair that came along with that. There were heavy sensations in his chest and a sense of gnawing emptiness in his stomach. He didn't fight these or try to change them. He noticed them with a kind of curiosity – exploring them, letting them be.

Moving his attention back to his breath, over and over, meta-awareness gradually entered his experience. He was noticing his thoughts, and deeply feeling his feelings, but at the same time he was able to stand back just a little. He allowed his experience just to be what it was – seeing the flow of thoughts, feelings and sensations as a flow of thoughts, feelings and sensations.

For a while that gave him some relief. But then his attention hooked onto the fresh scars on his stomach that followed his surgery. He noticed how this shaped and constricted his attention, so he moved his attention more deliberately to his breath – stepping back and allowing once more.

Opening his eyes, his attention broadened to take in both the sensations of breathing and the beautiful view from his window. There were snow-capped mountains on the horizon. Resting with that spacious expansiveness, Jacob began to re-appraise his circumstances. Rather than feeling doomed, he saw how lucky he was being alive. For a time he was filled with feelings of relief and contentment.

Soon after this, while dealing with paperwork from the hospital, he became distressed again: 'What if the cancer recurs?' He turned once more to his practice, noticing and allowing the feelings of fear that were running through his body. Acknowledging these, and coming back to the breath, he stood back again from the thoughts of recurrence. In a state of mindful awareness, he watched the fear-filled thoughts and anxious feelings dissipate. 'Like clouds dissolving into mist,' he said.

Feelings of being more at ease with things arose. That changed to an even more positive and buoyant state as his gaze settled on the photograph of his grandchildren propped by his bed. Enjoying the picture of their smiling faces, he thought: 'Cancer or no cancer, I still have so much I want to share with them.'

His attention broadened further, moving on to other positive aspects of his past and present circumstances: his long marriage to a loving partner, his professional accomplishments, and the various activities that he loved. Savouring the positive emotions that came with these moments of contemplation, he thought to himself, 'Cancer has strengthened my gratitude muscle.' Those thoughts matured into feelings of deep thankfulness and joy, along with the impulse to give more time and energy to his family. All of this enhanced his sense of happiness, meaningfulness and purpose.

This story, a true account adapted from the psychological literature on mindfulness, gives us important clues about how AIM can play a key part in the generation of happiness and well-being.[5]

What we saw with Vidyamala's story is how unwise reactions make us unhappier, while wise responses can tone down and even eliminate the secondary suffering that follows the unwanted experiences life delivers. Despite experiencing constant pain, Vidyamala says she is flourishing.

Jacob's story develops this theme and points towards strategies we can use to enhance our own happiness so that we too may come to flourish. Over the course of a few hours, Jacob – lying in his hospital bed – went on a kind of journey. Emotionally, it contained several ups and downs. But, despite the dips and constraints he experienced, the process that unfolded for him was one of gradually increasing positivity. AIM played a huge part in that – as did his ability to savour those positives.

So:

- When difficult and challenging experiences arise, AIM to step ever so slightly back. Don't react. Pause and notice. Explore and allow the unwanted elements of the experience to simply be what they are. Let what is the case be the case. Notice how your thoughts are affected by the experience. Explore how it is affecting your feelings and the sensations in your body. Give yourself the time to begin to come to terms with the experience.
- Allowing the fact that much of the experience will have a negative tone, notice too that there may be elements in your current experience that are actually positive. Once you have allowed what is unwanted, turn towards any positive elements and savour these. Allow that savouring process to begin to flavour your experience. Even though the experience might initially have come to you as powerfully unwanted, it needn't stay that way.
- With meta-awareness, notice when you fall into over-estimating the negative elements in the experience. Are there patterns of thinking and feeling that habitually recur? Can you smile at some of these? 'Oh yes, that's me – doing my disaster scenario again.'

Our combined experience, teaching Mind Time to thousands of people over the years, tells us that when we can AIM we become more alive. We become less reactive and more responsive. We're able to take in more of life's texture and richness. We become more fully present to our experience. When we're with another person, we're with them more fully. When we're outside in nature, we're in nature more fully. When we're doing any activity, we're more present and more able to become absorbed in it. That means we are much better placed to notice and to savour the positive elements in our experience.

When you can AIM you're more present. When you're more present, you're better able to savour the positive. When you can step back and savour the positive, even just a little, as Jacob found in his hospital bed, then even potentially catastrophic change can be an occasion for growth and development.

Events in the world spin on completely outside our control. We don't know what we will experience next. One thing we can be sure of, though, is that some of what is coming our way is going to be what we want – and some of it isn't.

There is a story from ancient India told about a king who found that walking on rough ground pained his delicate feet. So he sent word that he wanted all the ground in his kingdom covered in leather. But there wasn't enough leather in his kingdom to do that, and that made him very angry. Fortunately, his subjects were saved from his wrath by a wise man who came up with another solution. They made him a pair of sandals. That way, wherever he trod, he walked on smooth leather.

We can't eliminate pain and the unwanted from the world, but with AIM we come to experience these differently. Rather than trying to eliminate pain from the world, AIM and the Mind Time practices that develop it can be like putting on a pair of sandals. The world stays the same, but we're much better able to cope with the pain and difficulty that will inevitably come our way.

KEY MESSAGES OF CHAPTER 8

- There are two kinds of suffering – primary and secondary. Primary suffering is inescapable. Life will always give us things we don't want. But we can amplify that, and add unnecessary further suffering, when we're unwilling to allow what is the case to be the case. AIM can help you to stop slipping into secondary suffering.
- Instead of unhelpfully *reacting* when things we don't want occur, we can learn to *respond* more wisely. AIM helps you to do that.
- We can build our own resilience by making connections, keeping things in proportion, accepting change, moving towards our goals (even by very small steps), looking for opportunities for self-discovery, nurturing a more positive self-view, keeping things in perspective, maintaining a hopeful outlook and taking care of ourselves. With each of these elements, AIM can play a key part.
- When we add a capacity for savouring the positive into the mix, we can become even more resilient.
- We can't eliminate suffering from the world. But we can build our capacity to be with what suffering comes our way much more resourcefully. We don't have to cover the whole world with leather. We can put on a pair of sandals.

The Beginning

At this point in the book you will have been working with some of the practices we've shared, building your ability to AIM. You will have seen for yourself, from the inside, how the mind really is a kind of liquid lens, always shifting and changing.

Everything begins in the mind. As it shifts and changes, so the world we experience shifts and changes, too. Taking Mind Time regularly, hopefully you're beginning to experience your capacity to take some initiative around those changes.

We hope you're beginning to discover how Allowing, Inquiry and Meta-Awareness help you to gently shape your mind so that the world you experience is richer, warmer and full of exciting possibility.

- **Allowing** what is the case to be the case just that bit more often.
- **Inquiring** and becoming that bit more interested in your own experience, others' experience, and the richness of the world around you.
- **Meta-aware** of the ever-changing flow of that experience just that bit more often.

We hope that you're finding more choice – that you're more responsive, less reactive, more of the time.

The key word is 'more'. Just that bit more. Don't aim for perfection, don't expect miracles. But 'more' would be wonderful. Because it all adds up. Over time, small changes become huge shifts.

Our minds are the key to unlocking the life we wish to lead. The state of our minds not only directly affects *our* happiness, learning, creativity and performance; it affects the happiness, learning, creativity and performance of those around us, our family, friends and colleagues. The state of our mind determines our experience of life and deeply influences the experiences those around us have.

By now you may be seeing that with just 10 minutes a day you really can change your mind – and that can change everything.

It's wonderful that you've started to shape your own mind. It is a lifetime's journey, but now you've begun. Don't stop here. Our own experiences and those of the people we have worked with show it's about to get a whole lot more interesting if you keep going!

The novelist Robert Louis Stevenson wrote: 'To travel hopefully is a better thing than to arrive, and the true success is to labour.'[1] Stevenson was echoing the sentiment of an earlier Taoist saying: 'The journey is the reward.'

We wish you a fulfilling journey. Travel with humility and hope.

About Our Research

There are apps, self-help books and courses which suggest that mindfulness practices such as Mind Time can help people become more resilient, focused and aware – qualities that many believe can make them more effective at work and live happier lives.

We were interested in the way Mind Time might affect the experience of the people we worked with at Ashridge Executive Education. If they attended one of our courses and took Mind Time regularly, what would change? Because we work with busy people who struggle to find time for Mind Time, we also wanted to know what was the minimum effort people needed to make to achieve results.

We collected our data from participants who attended three half-day workshops at fortnightly intervals, as well as a full-day workshop and a final facilitated conference call with us. We taught them Mind Time practices, discussed the implication of these, and assigned home practices of daily Mind Time and other exercises for every day that the course ran. We recorded the trials and tribulations of our participants' attempts to learn to be mindful throughout the process.

We divided the participants into two groups and we asked both groups to complete a series of questionnaires, examining things such as their resilience, their levels of anxiety, their capacity to be aware of their experience, and their interpersonal skills.

We then took the first group through the programme and asked them to practise Mind Time at home every day. They were given audio recordings to help them do this. We measured both groups again after eight weeks – half of them had done the programme at this point and the other half had not.

We analysed the results and how they differed between the groups. The second group was our 'control group' and their results allowed us to take out any influence that simply the passage of time had on any improvements that were shown. That enabled us to focus more precisely on the effect that the training programme had. The second group subsequently took part in the same training.

Alongside the statistical analysis, we also recorded the participants talking about their experiences of Mind Time: what they found tricky and what they felt were benefits; how and when they practised; and what got in the way. Altogether there were 27 hours' worth of conversation and interviews, giving us rich data with which to understand what lay behind some of the statistical results we were finding.

We found that the more Mind Time each participant undertook, the greater the improvement in their scores on many measures including resilience, collaboration, agility, empathy, perspective taking and overall mindfulness. Crucially, those who practised for 10 minutes or more per day showed significant increases in resilience and overall mindfulness in comparison to those who practised less than 10 minutes daily.

Our research also points to some of the challenges that get in the way. First, people seek out practices such as Mind Time as a solution to their crushing work pressures, their busy timetables, their multiple task lists, and yet it is precisely these things that then get in the way of their practice. 'Busyness' and a focus on what needed to be done in the short term was one of the most commonly cited reasons for lack of practice. The people in our research who made real changes determinedly broke through that self-defeating cycle of pressure.

But, and again ironically, the research found that participants frequently berated themselves for their lack of practice. They felt guilty and even anxious. 'I'm bloody stressed about this mindfulness!' one exasperated person confided. As they piled pressure on themselves, some began to dislike practice and a few finally resisted altogether. But most of them kept going, and the benefits they discovered inform the contents of this book.

When you're trying to develop a new habit, including Mind Time, help and support from others is hugely valuable, and some in the research study received generous encouragement from their partners and their work colleagues. In moments where they might have given up, this support sustained them.

The reality is that, like becoming fitter, becoming more mindful involves some kind of training. That means you have to practise. Giving up 1 per cent of your time, though, is a small price to pay for the improvements that are on offer.

About the Authors

MICHAEL CHASKALSON

I was born and grew up in South Africa under apartheid. As soon as I could, I left there and, at 18, came to live in England. All the time I was growing up I was bothered by some philosophical questions. Issues like: 'What does it mean to be good?' 'How should I best live my life?' 'What is the real source of happiness?' Trying to find answers, I went to the University of East Anglia in Norwich to study philosophy. That didn't help. British academic philosophy in the 1970s had other interests. But just as I was graduating, one of my tutors – understanding my concerns – introduced me to an English Buddhist who had come to town to set up a new Buddhist Centre. He taught me to meditate, listened to my questions, didn't answer any of them, and that was it: I was hooked.

I felt that by pursuing the practice of meditation, by holding my questions ever more deeply, I might find some answers. So that's what I did. I spent the next 30 or so years engaged full-time in Buddhist activity, living communally with others in urban Buddhist centres or rural retreat centres practising meditation and studying Buddhist theory.

At 25 I had an excursion into business. A friend who was setting up social work projects with very deprived Indian Buddhists asked me if I'd help him raise funds for the work he was doing. We decided that I'd set up a fair-trade company in the UK, selling (both retail and wholesale) goods they provided from India and sending some of the profits back to India to fund his work.

The business went through many changes. Some of it was very stressful, but over time it grew and came to thrive. At its peak, it was employing a couple of hundred people, making sales of £10 million a year and giving away around £1 million a year to charitable causes. But running a business wasn't where my heart lay at the time so I went back full-time to meditating, studying and, eventually, teaching and writing about Buddhism: living the simple life.

In 2003, I decided it was time to make another change. I wanted to engage in the wider world once more, not just with people who came to Buddhist centres, and I looked for something that would enable me to do that. Mindfulness was just entering the clinical arena in the UK and people were beginning to be trained to use it in healthcare. So I joined the world's first Master's degree programme in mindfulness, which was teaching the clinical aspects of the practice.

I was the first graduate from that programme – the world's first 'master' in mindfulness. (Whatever else happens in my life, that's my claim to fame!) I also taught on the programme for several years.

From working with mental health professionals it was a short step to teaching mindfulness to executive coaches. They in turn introduced me to the organisations they worked in, and gradually more and more of my work came to centre on teaching mindfulness in organisations – mainly at senior levels.

I was back full-circle to that early interest in business.

Now I teach at business schools and run a mindfulness consultancy. It's a very different life from my earlier days as a quasi-monk

– but just as rewarding. I married Annette – my wonderful partner of many years. I have step-daughters, sons-in-law and four delightful grandchildren. I travel, teach and write. And I practise Mind Time. Even after all these years of doing it, it's still the bedrock for me.

In the more than 40 years since the mid-1970s when I first began to engage in mindfulness practice, it has exploded into popular culture in ways that many of us wished but few of us ever predicted. The challenge now is to ensure that it stays somehow true to its deepest roots while also helping as many people as possible.

My fervent hope for this book is that we can help people to see that the practices on offer aren't exotic and only for a few highly specialised and highly trained initiates. At the same time, I hope that as you practise them you'll see that they can go very deep indeed. I'm very conscious of what a privilege and responsibility it is to help someone take the first steps on a journey that can be completely life changing. If you've now begun to practise – keep going. There's so much more to discover!

MEGAN REITZ

In my last year at university in Cambridge, when all my friends were finding jobs, I had no idea what I wanted to do with my life. So I went backpacking for a year and a half to 'find myself'.

My father, a dairy farmer, and my mother, a teacher, had given me a sense that you should be passionate about the work and the path you chose through life.

I saw the Taj Mahal, learned to dive in Thailand, sold oil paintings from the back of a station wagon in Australia, bungee-jumped in New Zealand, went trekking in Bolivia and read mystical texts in Peru.

But I didn't find myself.

Instead, I did something you do when you're not sure what you want to do – I became a management consultant. I worked and played hard and ended up at boo.com – the epitome of the Internet boom in the late 1990s. At the age of 26 I found myself leading a global team with confident naivety and jet-setting around the world. Then the company, at one point estimated to be worth $500 million, crashed, burned and folded.

Despite the complete loss of the value of my shares in the company, despite getting no pay for my final weeks there, the financial loss didn't bother me too much. I realised that that wasn't what gave work – or life – meaning for me. But I still wasn't sure what did.

I went off again – to 'find myself'.

This time I travelled to Central America. I experienced no epiphany. But, miraculously, i did meet my future husband, Steve – in Guatemala. I now had a partner who was, and is, resolutely supportive.

On my return, I joined another management consultancy, learning how to apply a formula for 'change management' in companies. But – increasingly – while working with organisations trying to force through change projects and restructures, I became aware of a sense of emptiness in myself and in others. The word that described many of the relationships I saw inside organisations was 'transactional'.

In 2002, an old friend and travelling companion invited me to a weekend workshop on mindfulness, facilitated by Michael. It was the beginnings of finding an answer to a question I had become absorbed with – personally and professionally. 'What most enables us to connect deeply and meaningfully with others, in life and at work?'

That was the start of an exploration of my personal capacity to 'be fully present' in life, rather than be consumed by planning, reminiscing, ruminating and day-dreaming. I wanted to *live* – fully, wholeheartedly, passionately and responsibly. And I wanted to inspire those around me to do the same.

Always driven to look for deeper understanding, I studied for a Master's degree at Surrey University, and then a Master's and a doctorate at Cranfield University, and became a business school professor at Ashridge Executive Education. I also went on silent retreats and began to train more formally in mindfulness meditation.

But it was the arrival of my two daughters, Mia and Lottie, that really changed me. The possibility of connection between human beings took on a much more intimate meaning. How could I be the best mother I was capable of?

It raised very immediate questions. If I return home from juggling work commitments, distracted and stressed, how does *my* inner state affect the way *they* experience the world? What am I teaching them, consciously and unconsciously, about how to relate to themselves and others? How to live their lives with purpose and meaning? How do I not get too down on myself when I don't live up to my own high ideals of being the perfect mother?

Over the years, I turned more and more to mindfulness meditation practices to tune in to how my thoughts and feelings influenced the way I responded to events around me. How they affected my relations with others.

In parallel, as I began to spend more time as a coach to business leaders, I wondered how they might develop the capacity to be more mindful in their actions. If they were more mindful, might they lead organisations which are more humane – and allow employees to connect with one another and flourish?

Since I started regularly taking Mind Time, I have learned so much more about what it takes to live a fulfilling life now – in *this* moment and the moments that are ahead. And I am optimistic – because it isn't that complicated.

Simple practices, practised every day, have helped me increasingly 'find myself'. As it turns out I didn't need to look far. I was here all the time in my body. Now I am here also in my mind.

Acknowledgements

We would like to thank everyone who has helped us with this book and the research that underpins it. In particular, we wish to thank the Ashridge Executive Education Research team at Hult International Business School, especially our co-researchers, Lee Waller and Sharon Olivier. Our thanks also to Grace Brown, Viktor Nilsson and Sam Wilkinson who provided vital assistance with the analysis of data and review of literature.

Carolyn Thorne at HarperThorsons, Erika Lucas at Ashridge, and Stuart Crainer and Des Dearlove at Thinkers50 gave invaluable support to us in the editing and publishing process.

We would also like to thank all those people who have attended our programmes and who took part in the research itself, for their encouragement and commitment. We wish them well as they continue to build their ability to AIM.

Finally, we would wholeheartedly like to thank Annette Chaskalson and Steve Reitz who, with great kindness and patience, read beyond the calls of duty. Their wise insight and advice helped the book to become much more readable and, we hope, very much more applicable to a wide variety of readers.

Further Resources

If you'd like to read further into the subject, or to engage in mindfulness practice in a more systematic way, Michael's book *Mindfulness in Eight Weeks: The Revolutionary Eight-Week Plan to Clear Your Mind and Calm Your Life* (HarperThorsons, 2014) is a good place to start.

If you would like to know more about our research, you can access our report via www.hult.com or from our own websites (see below), and you can read our articles in the *Harvard Business Review*, www.hbr.org.

If you're interested in finding out more about how mindfulness practice can help with chronic pain and illness, Vidyamala Burch has much wisdom to share. At http://www.vidyamala-burch.com you can find out about her, the Breathworks organisation she founded and her books.

Ruby Wax's book *A Mindfulness Guide for the Frazzled* is a witty account of how we can use practices like those we've shared here to help deal with our crazy world today. You can find out more about her and her work at http://www.rubywax.net.

To find out more about how some of the ideas and practices we have discussed can help with issues such as depression, we recommend *The Mindful Way Through Depression: Freeing Yourself from*

Chronic Unhappiness (Guilford, 2007) by Mark Williams, John Teasdale and Zindel Segal.

If you'd like to know more about how we can help you to bring this kind of training to your workplace, see www.mbsr.co.uk and www.meganreitz.com.

References

Introduction

1. Micheva, K.D., Busse, B., Weiler, N.C., O'Rourke, N., and Smith, S.J. (2010), Single-synapse analysis of a diverse synapse population: proteomic imaging methods and markers. *Neuron* 68 (4), 639–53.
2. Killingsworth, M., and Gilbert, D. (2010), A wandering mind is an unhappy mind. *Science* 330 (6006), 932.
3. Ophir, E., Nass, C., and Wagner, A.D., (2009), Cognitive control in media multitaskers. *PNAS*106 (37) 15583–15587.

Chapter 1: Why AIM?

1. http://www.independent.co.uk/life-style/health-and-families/health-news/adults-uk-under-sleeping-health-sleep-fatigue-a6963631.html.
2. See action research methods, for example Judi Marshall (2016), *First Person Action Research* (Sage Publications).
3. Reitz, M., and Higgins, J. (2017), Being silenced and silencing others: developing the capacity to speak truth to power. Hult Research Report. Available at https://www.ashridge.org.uk/faculty-research/research/current-research/research-projects/speaking-truth-to-power/. See also Reitz, M., and Higgins, J.

(2017), The problem with saying my door is always open. *Harvard Business Review* online. Available at https://hbr. org/2017/03/the-problem-with-saying-my-door-is-always-open.

Chapter 2: Learning to AIM

1. http://www.jad-journal.com/article/0165-0327(94)00092-N/abstract.
2. https://today.duke.edu/2016/03/koh.
3. Lazar, S.W., *et al.* (2005), Meditation experience is associated with increased cortical thickness. *Neuroreport* 16(17), 1893–7.
4. Hölzel, B.K., Carmody, J., Vangel, M., Congleton, C., Yerramsetti, S.M., Gard, T., and Lazar, S.W. (2011), Mindfulness practice leads to increases in regional brain gray matter density. *Psychiatry Research* 191(1), 36–43.
5. Farb, N.A., *et al.*, 'Attending to the present: mindfulness meditation reveals distinct neural modes of self-reference', *SCAN*, vol. 2 (2007), 313–22.
6. Watson, N., *et al.* (2015), Recommended amount of sleep for a healthy adult: a joint consensus statement of the American Academy of Sleep Medicine and Sleep Research Society. *Journal of Clinical Sleep Medicine* 11, 591–2.

Chapter 3: AIM for Better Relationships

1. http://content.time.com/time/health/article/0,8599,2006938,00.html.
2. https://www.mentalhealth.org.uk/sites/default/files/the_lonely_society_report.pdf.
3. http://www.acas.org.uk/media/pdf/j/m/Flexible-working-and-work-life-balance.pdf.
4. https://hbr.org/2017/04/a-new-more-rigorous-study-confirms-the-more-you-use-facebook-the-worse-you-feel.
5. See *I'm OK, You're OK* by Thomas Anthony Harris (1967), which details the psychiatrist Eric Berne's thinking.

6. Adapted from Google's Search Inside Yourself Leadership Programme.
7. Inspired by Barbara Fredrickson (2014), *Love 2.0: Finding Happiness and Health in Moments of Connection* (Plume) and also Megan Reitz (2015), *Dialogue in Organizations: Developing Relational Leadership* (Palgrave Macmillan).
8. http://edition.cnn.com/2017/04/12/health/compassion-happiness-training/.
9. Stephen Covey (1989), *Seven Habits of Highly Effective People* (Free Press).
10. See The Ladder of Inference in Peter Senge (1990), *The Fifth Discipline* (Doubleday).
11. http://www.bbc.co.uk/news/science-environment-28512781.
12. Nancy Klein (2002), *Time to Think: Listening to Ignite the Human Mind* (Cassell).
13. Hatfield, E., Cacioppo, J.T., and Rapson, R.L. (1993), Emotional contagion. *Current Directions in Psychological Sciences* 2(3), 96–100.

Chapter 4: AIM for Happiness

1. Thanks to Jack Kornfield for this idea. Jack Kornfield (2011), *A Lamp in the Darkness: Illuminating the Path Through Difficult Times* (Sounds True Inc.), p.7.
2. Brickman, P., Coates, D., and Janoff-Bulman, R. (1978), Lottery winners and accident victims: is happiness relative? *Journal of Personality and Social Psychology* 36(8), 917–27.
3. Davidson, R.J., *et al.* (2003), Alterations in brain and immune function produced by mindfulness meditation. *Psychosomatic Medicine* 65, 564–70.
4. Sutton, S.K., and Davidson, R.J. (1997), Prefrontal brain asymmetry: a biological substrate of the behavioral approach and inhibition systems. *Psychological Science* 8 (3), 204–10.

5. Urry, H., *et al.* (2004), Making a life worth living: the neural correlates of well-being. *Psychological Science* 15(6), 367–72.

6. Davidson, R.J., *et al.* (2003), Alterations in brain and immune function produced by mindfulness meditation. *Psychosomatic Medicine* 65, 564–70.

7. R. Hanson (2009), *Buddha's Brain* (New Harbinger).

8. Baumeister, R.F., Finkenauer, C., and Vohs, K.D. (2001), Bad is stronger than good. *Review of General Psychology* 5(4), 323–70.

9. Fredrickson, B.L. (2013), Updated thinking on positivity ratios. *American Psychologist* 68(9), 814–22.

10. Ibid.

11. Barbara Fredrickson (2010), *Positivity* (Oneworld).

12. Ibid.

13. Johnson, K.J. and Fredrickson, B.L. (2005), Positive emotions eliminate the own-race bias in face perception. *Psychological Science* 16, 875–81.

14. Rowe, G.J., Hirsch, J.B., and Anderson, A.K. (2007), Positive affect increases the breadth of attentional selection. *Proceedings of the National Academy of Sciences of the United States of America* 104, 383–8.

15. Fredrickson, B.L., and Joiner, T. (2002), Positive emotions trigger upward spirals toward emotional well-being. *Psychological Science* 13 (2), 172–5.

16. Fredrickson, B.L. (2013), Updated thinking on positivity ratios. *American Psychologist* 68(9), 814–22.

17. Emmons, R.A., and McCullough, M.E. (2003), Counting blessings versus burdens: an experimental investigation of gratitude and subjective well-being in daily life. *Journal of Personality and Social Psychology* 84, 377–89.

18. Williams, L.A., and DeSteno, D. (2008), Pride and perseverance: the motivational role of pride. *Journal of Personality and Social Psychology* 94(6), 1007–17.

19. Fredrickson, B.L., *et al.* (2008), Open hearts build lives: positive emotions, induced through loving-kindness meditation, build consequential personal resources. *Journal of Personality and Social Psychology* 95(5), 1045–62.

Chapter 5: AIM for Effective Work
1. http://www.usatoday.com/story/money/2016/10/17/job-juggle-real-many-americans-balancing-two-even-three-gigs/92072068/.
2. https://www.ft.com/content/e32e13b2-a32b-11e4-bbef-00144feab7de.
3. http://www.radicati.com/wp/wp-content/uploads/2015/02/Email-Statistics-Report-2015-2019-Executive-Summary.pdf.
4. http://www.ccl.org/wp-content/uploads/2015/04/AlwaysOn.pdf.
5. ibid.
6. Megan Reitz (2015), *Dialogue in Organizations: Developing Relational Leadership* (Palgrave Macmillan).
7. http://www.usatoday.com/story/money/business/2013/06/08/countries-most-vacation-days/2400193/.
8. https://hbr.org/2015/04/why-some-men-pretend-to-work-80-hour-weeks.
9. K. Ashby and M. Mahdon (2010), *Why Do Employees Come to Work When Ill? An Investigation into Sickness Presence in the Workplace* (The Work Foundation).
10. http://www.thelancet.com/journals/lancet/article/PIIS0140-6736(15)60295-1/fulltext.
11. https://www.washingtonpost.com/news/on-leadership/wp/2015/08/24/working-more-than-55-hours-a-week-is-bad-for-you-in-many-ways/?tid=a_inl&utm_term=.760fd664bb74.
12. http://ftp.iza.org/dp8129.pdf.
13. http://www.danielgilbert.com/KILLINGSWORTH%20&%20GILBERT%20(2010).pdf

14. https://www.steelcase.com/insights/articles/making-distance-disappear/?utm_source=Social+Media&utm_medium=Twitter.
15. https://www.atlassian.com/time-wasting-at-work-infographic.
16. Ibid.
17. http://www.dailymail.co.uk/femail/article-2298347/Supermums-Two-thirds-mothers-admit-multi-tasking-EVERY-waking-hour-new-survey-reveals.html.
18. http://edition.cnn.com/2005/WORLD/europe/04/22/text.iq/.
19. Stephen Covey (1989), *Seven Habits of Highly Effective People* (Free Press).
20. Jeff Immelt, in a letter to General Electric shareholders, https://www.ge.com/ar2014/ceo-letter/.
21. http://www.claesjanssen.com/four-rooms/index.shtml.
22. Martin Buber (1937), *I and Thou*.
23. https://www.weforum.org/agenda/2016/11/70-of-employees-say-they-are-disengaged-at-work-heres-how-to-motivate-them/.
24. https://www.psychologicalscience.org/news/releases/im-bored-research-on-attention-can-help-us-understand-the-unengaged-mind.html.
25. Clance, P.R., and Imes, S.A. (1978). The imposter phenomenon in high achieving women: dynamics and therapeutic intervention. *Psychotherapy: Theory, Research and Practice.* 15 (3): 241–247. doi:10.1037/h0086006.
26. https://www.forbes.com/sites/amymorin/2016/01/30/5-surefire-signs-youre-dealing-with-a-psychopath/#7ce37cb962f6.
27. Ibid.
28. http://www.telegraph.co.uk/news/2016/09/13/1-in-5-ceos-are-psychopaths-australian-study-finds/.
29. http://www.telegraph.co.uk/women/work/imposter-syndrome-why-do-so-many-women-feel-like-frauds/.

Chapter 6: AIM for Better Health

1. http://www.who.int/topics/physical_activity/en/.

2. http://bjsm.bmj.com/content/43/1/1.

3. Tsafou, K.E. *et al.* (2015), Mindfulness and satisfaction in physical activity: a cross-sectional study in the Dutch population. *Journal of Health Psychology* 21(9), 1817–27.

4. Erisman, S.M., and Roemer, L. (2010), A preliminary investigation of the effects of experimentally induced mindfulness on emotional responding to film clips. *Emotion* 10(1), 72–82.

5. Jislin-Goldberg, T., Tanay, G., and Bernstein, A. (2012), Mindfulness and positive affect: cross-sectional, prospective intervention, and real-time relations. *Journal of Positive Psychology* 7(5), 349–61.

6. Baldwin, A.S., Baldwin, S.A., and Loehr, V.G. (2013), Elucidating satisfaction with physical activity: an examination of the day-to-day associations between experiences with physical activity and satisfaction during physical activity initiation. *Psychology & Health* 28(12), 1424–41.

7. Ulmer, C.S., Stetson, B.A., and Salmon, P.G. (2010), Mindfulness and acceptance are associated with exercise maintenance in YMCA exercisers. *Behaviour Research and Therapy* 48(8), 805–9.

8. http://www.nhs.uk/Livewell/fitness/Pages/physical-activity-guidelines-for-adults.aspx.

9. Sack, R., *et al.* (2007), Circadian rhythm sleep disorders: Part 1, Basic principles, shift work and jetlag disorders. *Sleep* 30, 1460–83.

10. Lanaj, K., Johnson, R., and Barnes, C. (2014), Beginning the working day yet already depleted? Consequences of late-night smartphone use and sleep. *Organizational Behaviour and Human Decision Processes* 124, 11–23.

11. Watson, N., *et al.* (2015), Recommended amount of sleep for a healthy adult: a joint consensus statement of the American Academy of Sleep Medicine and Sleep Research Society. *Sleep* 38, 843–4.

12. https://www.ashridge.org.uk/getmedia/26b590f7-dd02-4491-8f0c-8dea0b70664a/Business-of-Sleep.pdf.

13. http://www.nhs.uk/Livewell/insomnia/Pages/insomniatips.aspx.

14. Ong, J.C., Shapiro, S.L., and Manber, R. (2008), Combining mindfulness meditation with cognitive-behavior therapy for insomnia: a treatment-development study. *Behavior Therapy* 39(2), 171–82.

15. Thanks to Elizabeth English for pointing this out.

16. K. Duff (2014), *The Secret Life of Sleep* (Oneworld Publications).

17. Hamzelou, J. (2012), Overeating now bigger global problem than lack of food. *New Scientist*, https://www.newscientist.com/article/dn23004-overeating-now-bigger-global-problem-than-lack-of-food/.

18. Pezzolesi, C., and Placko, I. (2015), *The Art of Mindful Eating: How to Transform Your Relationship with Food and Start Eating Mindfully* (CreateSpace).

19. http://www.ejcr.org/publicity/April_2016/April2016Release2.pdf.

20. http://www.telegraph.co.uk/news/2017/04/16/day-prince-harry-showed-world-talk-problems/.

Chapter 7: AIM for Better Work–Life Balance

1. https://www.mentalhealth.org.uk/a-to-z/w/work-life-balance.

2. Yerkes, R.M., and Dodson, J.D. (1908), The relation of strength of stimulus to rapidity of habit-formation. *Journal of Comparative Neurology and Psychology* 18, 459–82.

3. https://www.mentalhealth.org.uk/a-to-z/w/work-life-balance.

4. https://www.deloitte.co.uk/mobileuk/.

5. https://www.deloitte.co.uk/mobileuk/better-living/.

6. http://www.telegraph.co.uk/technology/mobile-phones/9646349/Smartphones-and-tablets-add-two-hours-to-the-working-day.html.

7. Ibid.

8. https://www.theguardian.com/lifeandstyle/2014/nov/07/ ten-tips-for-a-better-work-life-balance.
9. Every day in the UK another 6,000 people take on a caring responsibility – over 2 million every year. See https:// www.carersuk.org/news-and-campaigns/press-releases/ facts-and-figures.
10. in the US about 44 million individuals will have provided a caring role for someone, perhaps an elderly relative, an ill partner or a child with a disability, in the previous 12 months. See http:// www.caregiving.org/caregiving2015/.
11. Half of all children in the US will live in a single-parent household before the age of 18. http://www.sciencedirect.com/science/ article/pii/S0090261616300705.

Chapter 8: AIMing When Times are Tough
1. https://www.everyday-mindfulness.org/interviews/interview-with-vidyamala-burch/.
2. V. King (2016), *10 Keys to Happier Living* (Headline).
3. A.S. Masten (2015), *Ordinary Magic: Resilience in Development* (Guilford Press).
4. http://www.apa.org/helpcenter/road-resilience.aspx.
5. We've adapted this story from one told by Eric Garland in Garland, E.L., Farb, N.A., Goldin, P.R., and Fredrickson, B.L. (2015), Mindfulness broadens awareness and builds eudaimonic meaning: a process model of mindful positive emotion regulation. *Psychological Inquiry* 26(4), 293–314.

The Beginning
1. Robert Louis Stevenson quotation, from *Virginibus Puerisque* (1881).

Index